THE FORC'D MARRIAGE;

or, the Jealous Bridegroom.

Va mon enfant! prends ta fortune.

PROLOGUE.

Gallants, our Poets have of late so us'd ye,
In Play and Prologue too so much abus'd ye,
That should we beg your aids, I justly fear,
Ye're so incens'd you'd hardly lend it here.
But when against a common Foe we arm,
Each will assist to guard his own concern.
Women those charming Victors, in whose Eyes
Lie all their Arts, and their Artilleries,
Not being contented with the Wounds they made,
Would by new Stratagems our Lives invade.
Beauty alone goes now at too cheap rates;
And therefore they, like Wise and Politick States,
Court a new Power that may the old supply,
To keep as well as gain the Victory.
They'll join the force of Wit to Beauty now,
And so maintain the Right they have in you.
If the vain Sex this privilege should boast,
Past cure of a declining Face we're lost.
You'll never know the bliss of Change; this Art
Retrieves (when Beauty fades) the wandring Heart;
And though the Airy Spirits move no more,
Wit still invites, as Beauty did before.
To day one of their Party ventures out,
Not with design to conquer, but to scout.
Discourage but this first attempt, and then
They'll hardly dare to sally out again.
The Poetess too, they say, has Spies abroad,
Which have dispersed themselves in every road,
I'th' Upper Box, Pit, Galleries; every Face
You find disguis'd in a Black Velvet Case.
My life on't; is her Spy on purpose sent,
To hold you in a wanton Compliment;
That so you may not censure what she 'as writ,
Which done, they face you down 'twas full of Wit.
Thus, while some common Prize you hope to win,
You let the Tyrant Victor enter in.
I beg to day you'd lay that humour by,
Till your Rencounter at the Nursery;
Where they, like Centinels from duty free,
May meet and wanton with the Enemy.

Enter an Actress.

How hast thou labour'd to subvert in vain,
What one poor Smile of ours calls home again?
Can any see that glorious Sight and say

[Woman pointing to the ladies.

A Woman shall not Victor prove to day?
Who is't that to their Beauty would submit,
And yet refuse the Fetters of their Wit?
He tells you tales of Stratagems and Spies;
Can they need Art that have such powerful Eyes?
Believe me, Gallants, he'as abus'd you all;
There's not a Vizard in our whole Cabal:
Those are but Pickeroons that scour for prey
And catch up all they meet with in their way;
Who can no Captives take, for all they do
Is pillage ye, then gladly let you go.
Ours scorns the petty Spoils, and do prefer
The Glory not the Interest of the War:
But yet our Forces shall obliging prove,
Imposing nought but Constancy in Love:
That's all our Aim, and when we have, it too,
We'll sacrifice it all to pleasure you.

ACT I.

SCENE I. The Palace.

Enter King, Philander, Orgulius, Alcippus, Alcander, Pisaro, Cleontius, Falatius; and Officers.

KING - How shall I now divide my Gratitude,
Between a Son, and one that has oblig'd me,
Beyond the common duty of a Subject?

PHILANDER - Believe me, Sir, he merits all your Bounty,
I only took example by his Actions;
And all the part o'th' Victory which I gain'd,
Was but deriv'd from him.

KING - Brave Youth, whose Infant years did bring us Conquests;
And as thou grew'st to Man, thou grew'st in Glory,
And hast arriv'd to such a pitch of it,
As all the slothful Youth that shall succeed thee,
Shall meet reproaches of thy early Actions:
When Men shall say, thus did the brave Alcippus;

The Forc'd Marriage by Aphra Behn
OR, THE JEALOUS BRIDEGROOM.

Aphra Behn was a prolific and well established writer but facts about her remain scant and difficult to confirm. What can safely be said though is that Aphra Behn is now regarded as a key English playwright and a major figure in Restoration theatre

Aphra was born into the rising tensions to the English Civil War. Obviously a time of much division and difficulty as the King and Parliament, and their respective forces, came ever closer to conflict.

There are claims she was a spy, that she travelled abroad, possibly as far as Surinam.

By 1664 her marriage was over (though by death or separation is not known but presumably the former as it occurred in the year of their marriage) and she now used Mrs Behn as her professional name.

Aphra now moved towards pursuing a more sustainable and substantial career and began work for the King's Company and the Duke's Company players as a scribe.

Previously her only writing had been poetry but now she would become a playwright. Her first, "The Forc'd Marriage", was staged in 1670, followed by "The Amorous Prince" (1671). After her third play, "The Dutch Lover", Aphra had a three year lull in her writing career. Again it is speculated that she went travelling again, possibly once again as a spy.

After this sojourn her writing moves towards comic works, which prove commercially more successful. Her most popular works included "The Rover" and "Love-Letters Between a Nobleman and His Sister" (1684–87).

With her growing reputation Aphra became friends with many of the most notable writers of the day. This is The Age of Dryden and his literary dominance.

From the mid 1680's Aphra's health began to decline. This was exacerbated by her continual state of debt and descent into poverty.

Aphra Behn died on April 16th 1689, and is buried in the East Cloister of Westminster Abbey. The inscription on her tombstone reads: "Here lies a Proof that Wit can never be Defence enough against Mortality." She was quoted as stating that she had led a "life dedicated to pleasure and poetry."

Index of Contents
ARGUMENT
SOURCE
THEATRICAL HISTORY
DRAMATIS PERSONAE
MEN
WOMEN
SCENE - Within the Court of FRANCE.
THE FORC'D MARRIAGE; or, the Jealous Bridegroom - PROLOGUE.
ACT I
SCENE I. The Palace.

SCENE II. Galatea's Apartments.
SCENE III. A Room in the House of Orgulius.
SCENE IV. Philander's Apartments.
ACT II
THE REPRESENTATIOPN OF THE WEDDING.
SCENE I. The Palace.
SCENE II. The Court Gallery.
SCENE III.
SCENE IV. Philander's Bed-chamber.
SCENE V. The Court Gallery.
SCENE VI.
SCENE VII. The Court Gallery.
ACT III
SCENE I. The Apartments of Alcippus.
SCENE II. The Palace.
SCENE III. Galatea's Apartments.
ACT IV
SCENE I. The Palace.
SCENE II. The Apartments of Alcippus.
SCENE III. The Court Gallery.
SCENE IV.
SCENE V. The Court Gallery.
SCENE VI. A Bed-chamber.
SCENE VII. The Palace.
SCENE VIII. The Gallery.
SCENE IX. Philander's Apartments.
ACT V
SCENE I. Galatea's Apartments.
SCENE II. The Bedchamber of Alcippus.
SCENE III. The King's Chamber.
SCENE IV. The Court Gallery.
SCENE V.
EPILOGUE
APHRA BEHN – A SHORT BIOGRAPHY
APHRA BEHN – A CONCISE BIBLIOGRAPHY
THE DORSET SQUARE THEATRE – A SHORT HISTORY

ARGUMENT

The King of France to reward his favourite Alcippus, at the motion of prince Philander, gladly assents to his being created general in place of old Orgulius, who seeks to resign his office, and further on his royal word pledges the new-made commander, Erminia, Orgulius' daughter, in marriage. The lady, however, loves the dauphin, whilst the princess Galatea is enamoured of Alcippus. All three are plunged into despair, and the brother and sister knowing each other's passion bemoan their hapless fate. The prince, indeed, threatens to kill Alcippus, upon which Galatea declares she will poniard Erminia. On the wedding night the bride confesses her love for Philander and refuses to admit Alcippus to her love. The dauphin at the same time serenades Erminia at her chamber door, but Pisaro, a friend to Alcippus, meeting him, there is a scuffle during which Alcander, the prince's companion, wounds the intruder. The noise rouses Erminia who issues from her room and encounters Philander.

Alcippus, seeing them together, mad with jealousy, attacks the prince. He is, however, beaten back and even wounded, and later his fury is inflamed by Pisaro's tale, who also informs the favourite that Galatea, for whom the narrator cherishes a hopeless love, dotes fondly upon him. Erminia, now that she has been joined in wedlock with Alcippus, guards herself carefully from the dauphin's passion, but when the general is obliged by his duties to leave for the camp Philander hopes to persuade her to yield to him. Alcippus, however, whose departure is a feint, returns secretly, leaving Pisaro to continue the journey alone. Isillia, Erminia's woman, has already admitted Philander to her mistress' chamber, when the lovers are surprised by the arrival of Alcippus on the scene. The prince is concealed, although the meeting had been purely innocent, but he is betrayed owing to the fact of his inadvertently leaving his hat and sword upon a table. He departs unmolested, but once he is gone Alcippus, beside himself with blind fury, strangles Erminia with an embroidered garter, Pisaro, coming in a few moments after, reproaches him with the murder but hurries him away to concealment. The deed, however, is discovered and noised abroad by Falatius, a busy coxcomb courtier. Orgulius demands Alcippus' life from the King, but Galatea, heart-broken, pleads for the man she loves. Philander is distraught with grief, and the King decides that if he harms himself Alcippus shall straightway pay the forfeit. The prince is about to wreak his vengeance on the cruel husband when he is met by Erminia herself, who, owing to her maid's attentions, has recovered from the swoon Alcippus took for death. It is resolved that Alcippus, who is now torn with agony and remorse, must be fittingly punished, and accordingly as he lies sick at heart in his chamber Erminia enters as a spirit, and so looking over his shoulder into a mirror wherein he is gazing tells him plainly of Galatea's love. The princess then passes by as it were a phantom, and after a masque, which he takes for a dream, he is conducted to a room draped in black wherein is placed a catafalque. Here he encounters Philander and as they are at hot words the King, who has been privy to the whole design, enters and the two are reconciled. Erminia next appears, and the happy accident explained, Erminia is bestowed upon the dauphin, whilst the princess is united to the favourite.

There is a slight underplot which deals with the amours of Aminta, sister to Pisaro, and Alcander. She is also courted by the cowardly fop, Falatius.

SOURCE

The Forc'd Marriage; or, The Jealous Bridegroom is the earliest, and most certainly one of the weakest of Mrs. Behn's plays. This is, however, far from saying that it is not a very good example of the Davenant, Howard, Porter, Stapylton school of romantic tragi-comedy. But Aphara had not yet hit upon her brilliant vein of intrigue. In The Forced Marriage she seems to have remembered The Maid's Tragedy. The situation between Alcippus and Erminia, Act ii, III, has some vague resemblance to that of Amintor and Evadne, Act ii, I. Aminta also faintly recalls Dula, whilst the song 'Hang love, for I will never pine' has a far-off echo of 'I could never have the power.' But Mrs. Behn has not approached within measuring distance of that supreme masterpiece.

THEATRICAL HISTORY

The stage history of The Forc'd Marriage; or, The Jealous Bridegroom is best told in the quaint phrase of old Downes. Produced in December, 1670 at the Duke's Theatre, Lincoln's Inn Fields, The

Jealous Bridegroom, says the veteran prompter, 'wrote by Mrs. Behn, a good play and lasted six days'. This, it must be remembered, was by no means a poor run at that time. 'Note,' continues the record, 'In this play, Mr. Otway the poet having an inclination to turn actor; Mrs. Behn gave him the King in this play for a probation part, but he being not us'd to the stage, the full house put him to such a sweat and tremendous agony, being dash'd, spoilt him for an actor.'

To quote Mr. Gosse's excellent and classic essay on Otway: 'The choice of the part showed the kindly tact of the shrewd Mrs. Behn. The king had to speak the few first words, to which the audience never listens, to make some brief replies in the first scene, and then not to speak again until the end of the fourth act. In the fifth act he had to make rather a long speech to Smith [Mr. Gosse by a slip writes 'Betterton'. The King (v, III) is talking to Philander, acted by Smith. Betterton played the favourite Alcippus.], explaining that he was "old and feeble, and could not long survive," and this is nearly all he had to say till the very end, where he was in great force as the kind old man who unites the couples and speaks the last words. It was quite a crucial test, and Otway proved his entire inability to face the public. He trembled, was inaudible, melted in agony, and had to leave the stage. The part was given to Westwood, a professional actor, and Otway never essayed to tread the boards again.'

The Forced Marriage seems never to have been revived since its production. On the title page of the second quarto (1690), The Forc'd Marriage is said to have been played at the Queen's Theatre. This is because the Duke's House temporarily changed its name thus. It does not refer to a second run of the play.

DRAMATIS PERSONAE

MEN
King.
Philander, his Son, betrothed to Erminia.
Alcippus, Favourite, in love with Erminia.
Orgulius, late General, Father to Erminia.
Alcander, Friend to the Prince, in love with Aminta.
Pisaro, Friend to the young General Alcippus.
Falatius, a fantastick Courtier.
Labree, his Man.
Cleontius, Servant to the Prince, and Brother to Isillia.,
Page to Pisaro.

WOMEN
Galatea, Daughter to the King.
Erminia, Daughter to Orgulius, espous'd to the Prince.
Aminta, Sister to Pisaro, in love with Alcander.
Olinda, Sister to Alcander, Maid of Honour to the Princess.
Isillia, Sister to Cleontius, Woman to Erminia.
Lysette, Woman to Aminta.
Clergy, Officers, Pages and Attendants.

SCENE - Within the Court of FRANCE.

And that great Name shall every Soul inspire
With Emulation to arrive at something,
That's worthy of Example.

ALCIPPUS - I must confess I had the honour, Sir,
To lead on twenty thousand fighting Men,
Whom Fortune gave the Glory of the Day to.
I only bid them fight, and they obey'd me;
But 'twas my Prince that taught them how to do so.

KING - I do believe Philander wants no courage;
But what he did was to preserve his own.
But thine the pure effects of highest Valour;
For which, if ought below my Crown can recompense,
Name it, and take it, as the price of it.

ALCIPPUS - The Duty which we pay your Majesty,
Ought to be such, as what we pay the Gods;
Which always bears its Recompence about it.

KING - Yet suffer me to make thee some return,
Though not for thee, yet to incourage Bravery.
I know thy Soul is generous enough,
To think a glorious Act rewards it self.
But those who understand not so much Virtue,
Will call it my neglect, and want of Gratitude;
In this thy Modesty will wrong thy King.
Alcippus, by this pause you seem to doubt
My Power or Will; in both you are to blame.

ALCIPPUS - Your pardon, Sir; I never had a thought
That could be guilty of so great a Sin.
That I was capable to do you service,
Was the most grateful Bounty Heaven allow'd me,
And I no juster way could own that Blessing,
Than to imploy the Gift for your repose.

KING - I shall grow angry, and believe your Pride
Would put the guilt off on your Modesty,
Which would refuse what that believes below it.

PHILANDER - Your Majesty thinks too severely of him;
Permit me, Sir, to recompense his Valour,
I saw the wonders on't, and thence may guess
In some Degree, what may be worthy of it.

KING - I like it well, and till thou hast perform'd it,
I will divest my self of all my Power,
And give it thee, till thou hast made him great.

PHILANDER - I humbly thank you, Sir.

[Bows to the King, takes the Staff from Orgulius, and gives it to Alcippus, who looks amazedly.

And here I do create him General.
You seem to wonder, as if I dispossess'd
The brave Orgulius; but be pleas'd to know,
Such Reverence and Respect I owe that Lord,
As had himself not made it his Petition,
I sooner should have parted with my Right,
Than have discharg'd my debt by injuring him.

KING - Orgulius, are you willing to resign it?

ORGULIUS - With your permission, Sir, most willingly;
His vigorous Youth is fitter for't than Age,
Which now has render'd me uncapable
Of what that can with more success perform.
My Heart and Wishes are the same they were,
But Time has quite depriv'd me of that power
That should assist a happy Conqueror.

KING - Yet Time has added little to your years,
Since I restor'd you to this great Command,
And then you thought it not unfit for you.

ORGULIUS - Sir, was it fit I should refuse your Grace?
That was your act of Mercy: and I took it
To clear my Innocence, and reform the Errors
Which those receiv'd who did believe me guilty,
Or that my Crimes were greater than that Mercy.
I took it, Sir, in scorn of those that hated me,
And now resign it to the Man you love.

KING - We need not this proof to confirm thy Loyalty;
Nor am I yet so barren of Rewards,
But I can find a way, without depriving
Thy noble Head of its victorious Wreaths,
To crown another's Temples.

ORGULIUS - I humbly beg your Majesty's consent to't,
If you believe Alcippus worthy of it;
The generous Youth I have bred up to Battles,
Taught him to overcome, and use that Conquest
As modestly as his submissive Captive,
His Melancholy, (but his easy Fetters)
To meet Death's Horrors with undaunted looks:
How to despise the Hardships of a Siege;
To suffer Cold and Hunger, want of Sleep.
Nor knew he other rest than on his Horse-back,
Where he would sit and take a hearty Nap;
And then too dreamt of fighting.

I could continue on a day in telling
The Wonders of this Warrior.

KING - I credit all, and do submit to you.
But yet Alcippus seems displeas'd with it.

ALCIPPUS - Ah, Sir! too late I find my Confidence
Has overcome my unhappy Bashfulness;
I had an humbler Suit to approach you with;
But this unlook'd for Honour
Has soon confounded all my lesser aims,
As were they not essential to my Being,
I durst not name them after what y'have done.

KING - It is not well to think my Kindness limited;
This, from the Prince you hold, the next from me;
Be what it will, I here declare it thine.
Upon my life, designs upon a Lady;
I guess it from thy blushing.
Name her, and here thy King engages for her.

PHILANDER - O Gods! What have I done?   [Aside.

ALCIPPUS - Erminia, Sir.   [Bows.

PHILANDER - I'm ruin'd.   [Aside.

KING - Alcippus, with her Father's leave, she's thine.

ORGULIUS - Sir, 'tis my Aim and Honour.

PHILANDER - Alcippus, is't a time to think of Weddings,
When the disorder'd Troops require your Presence?
You must to the Camp to morrow.

ALCIPPUS - You need not urge that Duty to me, Sir.

KING - A Day or two will finish that affair,
And then we'll consummate the happy Day,
When all the Court shall celebrate your Joy.

[They all go out, but Alcander, Pisaro and Falatius.

PISARO - Falatio, you are a swift Horseman;
I believe you have a Mistress at Court,
You made such haste this Morning.

FALATIUS - By Jove, Pisaro, I was weary enough of the
Campaign; and till I had lost sight of it,
I clapt on all my Spurs
But what ails Alcander?

PISARO - What, displeas'd?

ALCANDER - It may be so, what then?

PISARO - Then thou mayst be pleas'd again.

ALCANDER - Why the Devil should I rejoice?
Because I see another rais'd above me;
Let him be great, and damn'd with all his Greatness.

PISARO - Thou mean'st Alcippus, who I think merits it.

ALCANDER - What is't that thou cal'st Merit?
He fought, it's true, so did you, and I,
And gain'd as much as he o'th' Victory,
But he in the Triumphal Chariot rode,
Whilst we ador'd him like a Demi-God.
He with the Prince an equal welcome found,
Was with like Garlands, though less Merit, crown'd.

FALATIUS - He's in the right for that, by Jove.

PISARO - Nay, now you wrong him.

ALCANDER - What's he I should not speak my sense of him?

PISARO - He is our General.

ALCANDER - What then?
What is't that he can do, which I'll decline?
Has he more Youth, more Strength, or Arms than I?
Can he preserve himself i'th' heat of the Battle?
Or can he singly fight a whole Brigade?
Can he receive a thousand Wounds, and live?

FALATIUS - Can you or he do so?

ALCANDER - I do not say I can; but tell me then,
Where be the Virtues of this mighty Man,
That he should brave it over all the rest?

PISARO - Faith, he has many Virtues, and much Courage;
And merits it as well as you or I:
Orgulius was grown old.

ALCANDER - What then?

PISARO - Why then he was unfit for't,
But that he had a Daughter that was young.

ALCANDER - Yes, he might have lain by,
Like rusty Armour, else,
Had she not brought him into play again;
The Devil take her for't.

FALATIUS - By Jove, he's dissatisfy'd with every thing.

ALCANDER - She has undone my Prince,
And he has most unluckily disarm'd himself,
And put the Sword into his Rival's hand,
Who will return it to his grateful Bosom.

PHILANDER - Why, you believe Alcippus honest.

ALCANDER - Yes, in your sense, Pisaro,
But do not like the last demand he made;
'Twas but an ill return upon his Prince,
To beg his Mistress, rather challeng'd her.

PISARO - His ignorance that she was so, may excuse him.

ALCANDER - The Devil 'twill, dost think he knew it not?

Pis. Orgulius still design'd him for Erminia;
And if the Prince be disoblig'd from this,
He only ought to take it ill from him.

ALCANDER - Too much, Pisaro, you excuse his Pride,
But 'tis the Office of a Friend to do so.

PISARO - 'Tis true, I am not ignorant of this,
That he despises other Recompence
For all his Services, but fair Erminia,
I know 'tis long since he resign'd his Heart,
Without so much as telling her she conquer'd;
And yet she knew he lov'd; whilst she, ingrate,
Repay'd his Passion only with her Scorn.

ALCANDER - In loving him, she'd more ingrateful prove
To her first Vows, to Reason, and to Love.

PISARO - For that, Alcander, you know more than I.

FALATIUS - Why sure Aminta will instruct her better,
She's as inconstant as the Seas and Winds,
Which ne'er are calm but to betray Adventurers.

ALCANDER - How came you by that knowledg, Sir?

FALATIUS - What a Pox makes him ask me that question now?   [Aside.

PISARO - Prithee, Alcander, now we talk of her,
How go the Amours 'twixt you and my wild Sister?
Can you speak yet, or do you tell your tale
With Eyes and Sighs, as you were wont to do?

ALCANDER - Faith, much at that old rate, Pisaro,
I yet have no incouragement from her
To make my Court in any other language.

PISARO - You'll bring her to't, she must be overcome,
And you're the fittest for her fickle Humour.

ALCANDER - Pox on't, this Change will spoil our making Love,
We must be sad, and follow the Court-Mode:
My life on't, you'll see desperate doings here;
The Eagle will not part so with his Prey;
Erminia was not gain'd so easily,
To be resign'd so tamely. But come, my Lord,
This will not satisfy our appetites,
Let's in to Dinner, and when warm with Wine,
We shall be fitter for a new Design.

[They go out. Falatius stays.

FALATIUS - Now am I in a very fine condition,
A comfortable one, as I take it:
I have ventur'd my Life to some purpose now;
What confounded luck was this, that he of all men
Living, should happen to be my Rival?
Well, I'll go visit Aminta, and see how
She receives me.
Why, where a duce hast thou dispos'd of   Enter Labree.
Thy self all this day? I will be bound to be
Hang'd if thou hast not a hankering after
Some young Wench; thou couldst never loiter
Thus else; but I'll forgive thee now, and prithee go to
My Lady Aminta's Lodgings; kiss her hand
From me; and tell her, I am just returned from
The Campain: mark that word, Sirrah.

LABREE - I shall, Sir, 'tis truth.

FALATIUS - Well, that's all one; but if she should
Demand any thing concerning me, (for
Love's inquisitive) dost hear? as to my Valour, or so,
Thou understand'st me; tell her
I acted as a man that pretends to the glory of
Serving her.

LABREE - I warrant you, Sir, for a Speech.

FALATIUS - Nay, thou mayst speak as well too much
As too little; have a care of that, dost hear?
And if she ask what Wounds I have, dost mind me?
Tell her I have many, very many.

LABREE - But whereabouts, Sir?

FALATIUS - Let me see, let me see; I know not where
To place them, I think in my Face.

LABREE - By no means, Sir, you had much better
Have them in your Posteriors: for then the Ladies
Can never disprove you; they'll not look there.

FALATIUS - The sooner, you Fool, for the Rarity on't.

LABREE - Sir, the Novelty is not so great, I assure you.

FALATIUS - Go to, y'are wicked;
But I will have them in my Face.

LABREE - With all my heart, Sir, but how?

FALATIUS - I'll wear a patch or two there, and I'll
Warrant you for pretending as much as any man;
And who, you Fool, shall know the fallacy?

LABREE - That, Sir, will all that know you, both in the
Court and Camp.

FALATIUS - Mark me, Labree, once for all; if thou takest
Delight continually thus to put me in mind of
My want of Courage, I shall undoubtedly
Fall foul on thee, and give thee most fatal proofs
Of more than thou expectest.

LABREE - Nay, Sir, I have done, and do believe 'tis only
I dare say you are a man of Prowess.

FALATIUS - Leave thy simple fancies, and go about thy business.

LABREE - I am gone; but hark, my Lord,
If I should say your Face were wounded,
The Ladies would fear you had lost your Beauty.

FALATIUS - O, never trouble your head for that, Aminta
Is a Wit, and your Wits care not how ill-favour'd
Their Men be, the more ugly the better.

LABREE - An't be so, you'll fit them to a hair.

FALATIUS - Thou art a Coxcomb, to think a man of my
Quality needs the advantage of Handsomness:
A trifle as insignificant as Wit or Valour; poor
Nothings, which Men of Fortune ought to despise.

LABREE - Why do you then keep such a stir, to gain
The reputation of this thing you so despise?

FALATIUS - To please the peevish humour of a Woman,
Who in that point only is a Fool.

LABREE - You had a Mistress once, if you have not
Forgotten her, who would have taken you with
All these faults.

FALATIUS - There was so; but she was poor, that's the Devil,
I could have lov'd her else.
But go thy ways; what dost thou muse on?

LABREE - Faith, Sir, I am only fearful you will never
Pass with those Patches you speak of.

FALATIUS - Thou never-to-be-reclaim'd Ass, shall I never
Bring thee to apprehend as thou ought'st? I tell thee,
I will pass and repass, where and how I please;
Know'st thou not the difference yet, between a Man
Of Money and Titles, and a Man of only Parts,
As they call them? poor Devils of no Mein nor Garb:
Well, 'tis a fine and frugal thing, this Honour,
It covers a multitude of Faults:
Even Ridicule in one of us is a-la-mode.
But I detain thee; go haste to Aminta.

[Exeunt severally.

SCENE II. Galatea's Apartments.

Enter Galatea, Aminta, and Olinda.

GALATEA - Will Erminia come?

OLINDA - Madam, I thought she'd been already here.

GALATEA - But prithee how does she support this news?

OLINDA - Madam, as those unreconciled to Heaven
Would bear the pangs of death.

AMINTA - Time will convince her of that foolish error,

Of thinking a brisk young Husband a torment.

GALATEA - What young Husband?

AMINTA - The General, Madam.

GALATEA - Why, dost thou think she will consent to it?

AMINTA - Madam, I cannot tell, the World's inconstant.

GALATEA - Ay, Aminta, in every thing but Love;
And sure they cannot be in that:
What say'st thou, Olinda?

OLINDA - Madam, my Judgment's naught.
Love I have treated as a stranger Guest,
Receiv'd him well, not lodg'd him in my Breast.
I ne'er durst give the unknown Tyrant room;
Lest he should make his resting place his home.

GALATEA - Then thou art happy; but if Erminia fail,
I shall not live to reproach her.

AMINTA - Nay, Madam, do not think of dying yet:
There is a way, if we could think of it.

GALATEA - Aminta, when will thou this Humour lose?

AMINTA - Faith, never, if I might my Humour chuse.

GALATEA - Methinks thou now should'st blush to bid me live.

AMINTA - Madam, 'tis the best counsel I can give.

GALATEA - Thy Counsel! Prithee, what dost counsel now?

AMINTA - What I would take my self I counsel you.

GALATEA - You must my Wounds and my Misfortunes bear
Before you can become my Counsellor.
You cannot guess the Torments I endure:
Not knowing the Disease you'll miss the Cure.

AMINTA - Physicians, Madam, can the Patient heal
Although the Malady they ne'er did feel;
But your Disease is epidemical,
Nor can I that evade that conquers all.
I lov'd, and never did like pleasure know,
Which Passion did with time less vigorous grow.

GALATEA - Why, hast thou lost it?

AMINTA - It, and half a score.

GALATEA - Losing the first, sure thou couldst love no more.

AMINTA - With more facility, than when the Dart
Arm'd with resistless fire first seiz'd my Heart;
'Twas long then e'er the Boy could entrance get,
And make his little Victory compleat;
And now he'as got the knack on't, 'tis with ease
He domineers, and enters when he please.

GALATEA - My Heart, Aminta, is not like to thine.

AMINTA - Faith, Madam, try, you'll find it just like mine.
The first I lov'd was Philocles, and then
Made Protestations ne'er to love again,
Yet after left him for a faithless crime;
But then I languisht even to death for him;
But Love who suffer'd me to take no rest,
New fire-balls threw, the old scarce dispossest;
And by the greater flame the lesser light,
Like Candles in the Sun extinguished quite,
And left no power Alcander to resist,
Who took, and keeps possession of my breast.

GALATEA - Art thou a Lover then, and look'st so gay,
But thou hast ne'er a Father to obey.   [Sighing.

AMINTA - Why, if I had I would obey him too.

GALATEA - And live?

AMINTA - And live.

GALATEA - 'Tis more than I can do.

Enter Erminia weeping.

Thy Eyes, Erminia, do declare thy Heart
[Gal. meets her, embraces her, and weeps.
Has nothing but Despairs and Death t'impart,
And I alas, no Comfort can apply,
But I as well as you can weep and die.

ERMINIA - I'll not reproach my Fortune, since in you
Grief does the noblest of your Sex subdue;
When your great Soul a sorrow can admit,
I ought to suffer from the sense of it;
Your cause of grief too much like mine appears,
Not to oblige my Eyes to double tears;

And had my heart no sentiments at home,
My part in yours had doubtless fill'd the room.
But mine will no addition more receive,
Fate has bestow'd the worst she had to give;
Your mighty Soul can all its rage oppose,
Whilst mine must perish by more feeble blows.

GALATEA - Indeed I dare not say my cause of grief
Does yours exceed, since both are past relief.
But if your Fates unequal do appear,
Erminia, 'tis my heart that odds must bear.

ERMINIA - Madam, 'tis just I should to you resign,
But here you challenge what is only mine:
My Fate so cruel is, it will not give
Leave to Philander (if I die) to live:
Might I but suffer all, 'twere some content,
But who can live and see this languishment?
You, Madam, do alone your Sorrows bear,
Which would be less, did but Alcippus share;
As Lovers we agree, I'll not deny,
But thou art lov'd again, so am not I.

AMINTA - Madam, that grief the better is sustain'd,
That's for a loss that never yet was gain'd;
You only lose a man that does not know
How great the honour is which you bestow;
Who dares not hope you love, or if he did,
Your Greatness would his just return forbid;
His humble thoughts durst ne'er to you aspire,
At most he would presume but to admire;
Or if it chanc'd he durst more daring prove,
You still must languish and conceal your Love.

GALATEA - This which you argue lessens not my Pain,
My Grief's the same were I belov'd again.
The King my Father would his promise keep,
And thou must him enjoy for whom I weep.

ERMINIA - Ah, would I could that fatal gift deny;
Without him you; and with him, I must die;
My Soul your royal Brother does adore,
And I, all Passion, but from him, abhor;
But if I must th'unsuit Alcippus wed,
I vow he ne'er shall come into my Bed.

GALATEA - That's bravely sworn, and now I love thee more
Than e'er I was oblig'd to do before,
But yet, Erminia, guard thee from his Eyes,
Where so much love, and so much Beauty lies;
Those charms may conquer thee, which made me bow,

And make thee love as well as break this Vow.

ERMINIA - Madam, it is unkind, though but to fear
Ought but Philander can inhabit here.
[Lays her hand on her heart.

GALATEA - Ah, that Alcippus did not you approve,
We then might hope these mischiefs to remove;
The King my Father might be won by Prayer,
And my too powerful Brother's sad despair,
To break his word, which kept will us undo:
And he will lose his dear Philander too,
Who dies and can no remedies receive:
But vows that 'tis for you alone he'll live.

ERMINIA - Ah, Madam, do not tell me how he dies,
I've seen too much already in his Eyes:
They did the sorrows of his Soul betray,
Which need not be confest another way:
'Twas there I found what my misfortune was,
Too sadly written in his lovely face.
But see, my Father comes: Madam, withdraw a while,
And once again I'll try my interest with him.

[Exeunt.

SCENE III. A Room in the House of Orgulius.

Enter Orgulius, Erminia weeping, and Isillia.

ERMINIA - Sir, does your fatal resolution hold?

ORGULIUS - Away, away, you are a foolish Girl,
And look with too much pride upon your Beauty;
Which like a gaudy flower that springs too soon,
Withers e'er fully blown.
Your very Tears already have betray'd
Its weak inconstant nature;
Alcippus, should he look upon thee now,
would swear thou wert not that fine thing he lov'd.

ERMINIA - Why should that blessing turn to my despair?
Curse on his Faith that told him I was fair.

ORGULIUS - 'Tis strange to me you shou'd despise this Fortune,
I always thought you well inclin'd to love him,
I would not else have thus dispos'd of you.

ERMINIA - I humbly thank you, Sir, though't be too late,

And wish you yet would try to change my Fate;
What to Alcippus you did Love believe,
Was such a Friendship as might well deceive;
'Twas what kind Sisters do to Brothers pay;
Alcippus I can love no other way.
Sir, lay the Interest of a Father by,
And give me leave this Lover to deny.

ORGULIUS - Erminia, thou art young, and canst not see
The advantage of the Fortune offer'd thee.

ERMINIA - Alas, Sir, there is something yet behind.   [Sighs.

ORGULIUS - What is't, Erminia? freely speak thy mind.

ERMINIA - Ah, Sir, I dare not, you inrag'd will grow.

ORGULIUS - Erminia, you have seldom found me so;
If no mean Passion have thy Soul possest,
Be what it will I can forgive the rest.

ERMINIA - No, Sir, it is no crime, or if it be,
Let Prince Philander make the Peace for me;
He 'twas that taught the Sin (if Love be such.)

ORGULIUS - Erminia, peace, he taught you then too much.

ERMINIA - Nay, Sir, you promis'd me you wou'd not blame
My early Love, if 'twere a noble Flame.

ORGULIUS - Than this a more unhappy could not be;
Destroy it, or expect to hear of me.
[Offers to go out.

ERMINIA - Alas, I know 'twould anger you, when known.
[She stays him.

ORGULIUS - Erminia, you are wondrous daring grown.
Where got you courage to admit his Love,
Before the King or I did it approve?

ERMINIA - I borrow'd Courage from my Innocence,
And my own Virtue, Sir, was my defence.
Philander never spoke but from a Soul,
That all dishonest Passions can controul;
With Flames as chaste as Vestals that did burn,
From whence I borrow'd mine, to make return.

ORGULIUS - Your Love from Folly, not from Virtue grew;
You never could believe he'd marry you.

ERMINIA - Upon my life no other thing he spoke,
But those from dictates of his Honour took.

ORGULIUS - Though by his fondness led he were content
To marry thee, the King would ne'er consent.
Cease then this fruitless Passion, and incline
Your Will and Reason to agree with mine,
Alcippus I dispos'd you to before,
And now I am inclin'd to it much more.
Some days I had design'd t'have given thee
To have prepar'd for this solemnity;
But now my second thoughts believe it fit,
You should this night to my desires submit.

ERMINIA - This night! Ah, Sir, what is't you mean to do?

ORGULIUS - Preserve my Credit, and thy Honour too.

ERMINIA - By such resolves you me to ruin bring.

ORGULIUS - That's better than to disoblige my King.

ERMINIA - But if the King his liking do afford,
Would you not with Alcippus break your word?
Or would you not to serve your Prince's life,
Permit your Daughter to become his Wife?

ORGULIUS - His Wife, Erminia! if I did believe
Thou could'st to such a thought a credit give,
I would the interest of a Father quit,
And you, Erminia, have no need of it:
Without his aid you can a Husband chuse;
Gaining the Prince you may a Father lose.

ERMINIA - Ah, Sir, these words are Poniards to my Heart;
And half my Love to Duty does convert;
Alas, Sir, I can be content to die,
But cannot suffer this Severity: [Kneels.
That care you had, dear Sir, continue still,
I cannot live and disobey your will.   [Rises.

ORGULIUS - This duty has regain'd me, and you'll find
A just return; I shall be always kind.
Go, reassume your Beauty, dry your Eyes;
Remember 'tis a Father does advise.   [Goes out.

ERMINIA - Ungrateful Duty, whose uncivil Pride
By Reason is not to be satisfy'd;
Who even Love's Almighty Power o'erthrows,
Or does on it too rigorous Laws impose;
Who bindest up our Virtue too too strait,

And on our Honour lays too great a weight.
Coward, whom nothing but thy power makes strong;
Whom Age and Malice bred t'affright the young;
Here thou dost tyrannize to that degree,
That nothing but my Death will set me free.

[Ex. Erminia and Isillia.

SCENE IV. Philander's Apartments.

Enter Philander and Alcander.

PHILANDER - Urge it no more, your Reasons do displease me;
I offer'd her a Crown with her Philander,
And she was once pleas'd to accept of it.
She lov'd me too, yes, and repaid my flame,
As kindly as I sacrific'd to her:
The first salute we gave were harmless Love,
Our Souls then met, and so grew up together,
Like sympathizing Twins.
And must she now be ravish'd from my Arms?
Will you, Erminia, suffer such a Rape?
What though the King have said it shall be so,
'Tis not his pleasure can become thy Law,
No, nor it shall not.
And though he were my God as well as King,
I would instruct thee how to disobey him;
Thou shalt, Erminia, bravely say, I will not;
He cannot force thee to't against thy will.
Oh Gods, shall duty to a King and Father
Make thee commit a Murder on thy self,
Thy sacred self, and me that do adore thee?
No, my Erminia, quit this vain devoir,
And follow Love that may preserve us all:
Presumptuous Villain, bold Ingratitude
Hadst thou no other way to pay my favours?
By Heaven, 'twas bravely bold, was it not, Alcander?

ALCANDER - It was somewhat strange, Sir;
But yet perhaps he knew not that you lov'd her.

PHILANDER - Not know it! yes, as well as thou and I.
The world was full on't, and could he be ignorant?
Why was her Father call'd from banishment,
And plac'd about the King, but for her sake?
What made him General, but my Passion for her?
What gave him twenty thousand Crowns a year,
But that which made me captive to Erminia,
Almighty Love, of which thou say'st he is ignorant?

How has he order'd his audacious flame,
That I cou'd ne'er perceive it all this while.

ALCANDER - Then 'twas a flame conceal'd from you alone,
To the whole Court, besides, 'twas visible.
He knew you would not suffer it to burn out;
And therefore waited till his services
Might give encouragement to's close design.
If that could do't he nobly has endeavour'd it,
But yet I think you need not yield her, Sir.

Phiander - Alcippus, I confess, is brave enough,
And by such ways I'll make him quit his claim;
He shall to morrow to the Camp again,
And then I'll own my Passion to the King;
He loves me well, and I may hope his pity.

Till then be calm, my Heart, for if that fail,
[Points to his Sword.
This is the argument that will prevail.

[Exeunt.

ACT II.

THE REPRESENTATION OF THE WEDDING.

The Curtain must be let down, and soft Musick must play: The Curtain being drawn up, discovers a scene of a Temple: The King sitting on a Throne, bowing down to join the hands Alcippus and Erminia, who kneel on the steps of the Throne; the Officers of the Court and Clergy standing in order by, with Orgulius. This within the Scene.

Without on the Stage, Philander with his Sword half drawn, held by Galatea, who looks ever on Alcippus: Erminia still fixing her Eyes on Philander; Pisaro passionately gazing on Galatea: Aminta on Fallatio, and he on her: Alcander, Isillia, Cleontius, in other several postures, with the rest, all remaining without motion, whilst the Musick softly plays; this continues a while till the Curtain falls; and then the Musick plays aloud till the Act begins.

SCENE I. The Palace.

Enter Philander and Galatea inrag'd.

PHILANDER - 'Tis done, 'tis done, the fatal knot is ty'd,
Erminia to Alcippus is a Bride;
Methinks I see the Motions of her Eyes,
And how her Virgin Breasts do fall and rise:
Her bashful Blush, her timorous Desire,
Adding new Flame to his too vigorous Fire;

Whilst he the charming Beauty must embrace,
And shall I live to suffer this Disgrace?
Shall I stand tamely by, and he receive
That Heaven of bliss, defenceless she can give?
No, Sister, no, renounce that Brother's name,
Suffers his Patience to surmount his Flame;
I'll reach the Victor's heart, and make him see,
That Prize he has obtain'd belongs to me.

GALATEA - Ah, dear Philander, do not threaten so,
Whilst him you wound, you kill a Sister too.

PHILANDER - Though all the Gods were rallied on his side,
They should too feeble prove to guard his Pride.
Justice and Honour on my Sword shall sit,
And my Revenge shall guide the lucky hit.

GALATEA - Consider but the danger and the crime,
And, Sir, remember that his life is mine.

PHILANDER - Peace, Sister, do not urge it as a sin,
Of which the Gods themselves have guilty been:
The Gods, my Sister, do approve Revenge
By Thunder, which th'Almighty Ports unhinge,
Such is their Lightning when poor Mortals fear,
And Princes are the Gods inhabit here;
Revenge has charms that do as powerful prove
As those of Beauty, and as sweet as Love,
The force of Vengeance will not be withstood,
Till it has bath'd and cool'd it self in Blood.
Erminia, sweet Erminia, thou art lost,
And he yet lives that does the conquest boast.

GALATEA - Brother, that Captive you can ne'er retrieve
More by the Victor's death, than if he live,
For she in Honour cannot him prefer,
Who shall become her Husband's Murderer;
By safer ways you may that blessing gain,
When venturing thus through Blood and Death prove vain.

PHILANDER - With hopes already that are vain as Air,
You've kept me from Revenge, but not Despair.
I had my self acquitted, as became
Erminia's wrong'd Adorer, and my Flame;
My Rival I had kill'd, and set her free,
Had not my Justice been disarm'd by thee.
But for thy faithless Hope, I 'ad murder'd him,
Even when the holy Priest was marrying them,
And offer'd up the reeking Sacrifice
To th'Gods he kneel'd to, when he took my price;
By all their Purity I would have don't.

But now I think I merit the Affront:
He that his Vengeance idly does defer,
His Safety more than his Success must fear:
I, like that Coward, did prolong my Fate,
But brave Revenge can never come too late.

GALATEA - Brother, if you can so inhuman prove
To me your Sister, Reason, and to Love:
I'll let you see that I have sentiments too,
Can love and be reveng'd as well as you;
That hour that shall a death to him impart,
Shall send this Dagger to Erminia's heart.
[Shews a Dagger.

PHILANDER - Ah, Coward, how these words have made thee pale,
And Fear above thy Courage does prevail:
Ye Gods, why did you such a way invent?

GALATEA - None else was left thy madness to prevent.

PHILANDER - Ah, cruel Sister, I am tame become,
And will reverse my happy Rival's doom:
Yes, he shall live to triumph o'er my Tomb.
But yet what thou hast said, I needs must blame,
For if my resolutions prove the same,
I now should kill thee, and my life renew;
But were it brave or just to murder you?
At worst, I should an unkind Sister kill,
Thou wouldst the sacred blood of Friendship spill.
I kill a Man that has undone my Fame,
Ravish'd my Mistress, and contemn'd my Name,
And, Sister, one who does not thee prefer:
But thou no reason hast to injure her.
Such charms of Innocence her Eyes do dress,
As would confound the cruel'st Murderess:
And thou art soft, and canst no Horror see,
Such Actions, Sister, you must leave to me.

GALATEA - The highest Love no Reason will admit,
And Passion is above my Friendship yet.

PHILANDER - Then since I cannot hope to alter thee,
Let me but beg that thou wouldst set me free;
Free this poor Soul that such a coil does keep;
'Twill neither let me wake in Peace, nor sleep.
Comfort I find a stranger to my heart,
Nor canst thou ought of that but thus impart;
Thou shouldst with joy a death to him procure,
Who by it leaves Alcippus' life secure.

GALATEA - Dear Brother, you out-run your Patience still,

We'll neither die our selves, nor others kill;
Something I'll do that shall thy joys restore,
And bring thee back that health thou had'st before;
We're now expected at the Banquet, where
I'd have thy Eyes more Love than Anger wear:
This night be cheerful, and on me depend,
On me, that am thy Sister, and thy Friend:
A little raise Alcippus' Jealousy
And let the rest be carried on by me;
Nor would it be amiss should you provide
A Serenade to entertain the Bride:
'Twill give him Fears that may perhaps disprove
The fond opinion of his happy Love.

PHILANDER - Though Hope be faithless, yet I cannot chuse,
Coming from thee, but credit the abuse.

GALATEA - Philander, do not your Hope's power distrust,
'Tis time enough to die, when that's unjust.

[Exeunt.

SCENE II. The Court Gallery.

Enter Aminta as passing over the Stage, is stayed by Olinda.

OLINDA - Why so hasty, Aminta?

AMINTA - The time requires it, Olinda.

OLINDA - But I have an humble suit to you.

AMINTA - You shall command me any thing.

OLINDA - Pray Heaven you keep your word.

AMINTA - That sad tone of thine, Olinda, has almost
Made me repent of my promise; but come, what is't?

OLINDA - My Brother, Madam.

AMINTA - Now fie upon thee, is that all thy business?
[Offers to go off.

OLINDA - Stay, Madam, he dies for you.

AMINTA - He cannot do't for any Woman living;
But well, it seems he speaks of Love to you;
To me he does appear a very Statue.

OLINDA - He nought but sighs and calls upon your name,
And vows you are the cruell'st Maid that breathes.

AMINTA - Thou can'st not be in earnest sure.

OLINDA - I'll swear I am, and so is he.

AMINTA - Nay, thou hast a hard task on't, to make
Vows to all the Women he makes love to;
Indeed I pity thee; ha, ha, ha.

OLINDA - You should not laugh at those you have undone.

Aminta sings.

Hang Love, for I will never pine
For any Man alive;
Nor shall this jolly Heart of mine
The thoughts of it receive;
I will not purchase Slavery
At such a dangerous rate;
But glory in my Liberty,
And laugh at Love and Fate.

OLINDA - You'll kill him by this cruelty.

AMINTA - What is't thou call'st so?
For I have hitherto given no denials,
Nor has he given me cause;
I have seen him wildly gaze upon me often,
And sometimes blush and smile, but seldom that;
And now and then found fault with my replies,
And wonder'd where the Devil lay that wit,
Which he believ'd no Judge of it could find.

OLINDA - Faith, Madam, that's his way of making love.

AMINTA - It will not take with me, I love a Man
Can kneel, and swear, and cry, and look submiss,
As if he meant indeed to die my Slave:
Thy Brother looks, but too much like a Conqueror.   [Sighs.

OLINDA - How, Aminta, can you sigh in earnest?

AMINTA - Yes, Olinda, and you shall know its meaning;
I love Alcander, and am not asham'd o'th' secret,
But prithee do not tell him what I say.
Oh, he's a man made up of those Perfections,
Which I have often lik'd in several men;
And wish'd united to compleat some one,

Whom I might have the glory to o'ercome.
His Mein and Person, but 'bove all his Humour,
That surly Pride, though even to me addrest,
Does strangely well become him.

OLINDA - May I believe this?

AMINTA - Not if you mean to speak on't,
But I shall soon enough betray my self.

Enter Falatius with a patch or two on his Face.

Falatius, welcome from the Wars;
I'm glad to see y'ave scap'd the dangers of them.

FALATIUS - Not so well scap'd neither, Madam, but I
Have left still a few testimonies of their
Severity to me.   [Points to his face.

OLINDA - That's not so well, believe me.

FALATIUS - Nor so ill, since they be such as render us
No less acceptable to your fair Eyes, Madam!
But had you seen me when I gain'd them, Ladies,
In that heroick posture.

AMINTA - What posture?

FALATIUS - In that of fighting, Madam;
You would have call'd to mind that antient story
Of the stout Giants that wag'd War with Heaven;
Just so I fought, and for as glorious prize,
Your excellent Ladiship.

AMINTA - For me, was it for me you ran this hazard then?

FALATIUS - Madam, I hope you do not question that,
Was it not all the faults you found with me,
The reputation of my want of Courage,
A thousand Furies are not like a Battle;
And but for you,
By Jove, I would not fight it o'er again
For all the glory on't; and now do you doubt me?
Madam, your heart is strangely fortified
That can resist th'efforts I have made against it,
And bring to boot such marks of valour too.

Enter to them Alcander, who seeing them would
turn back, but Olinda stays him.

OLINDA - Brother, come back.

FALATIUS - Advance, advance, what, Man, afraid of me?

ALCANDER - How can she hold discourse with that Fantastick.   [Aside.

FALATIUS - Come forward, and be complaisant.   [Pulls him again.

ALCANDER - That's most proper for your Wit, Falatius.

AMINTA - Why so angry?

ALCANDER - Away, thou art deceiv'd.

AMINTA - You've lost your sleep, which puts you out of humour.

ALCANDER - He's damn'd will lose a moment on't for you.

AMINTA - Who is't that has displeas'd you?

ALCANDER - You have, and took my whole repose away,
And more than that, which you ne'er can restore;
I can do nothing as I did before.
When I would sleep, I cannot do't for you,
My Eyes and Fancy do that form pursue;
And when I sleep, you revel in my Dreams,
And all my Life is nothing but extremes.
When I would tell my love, I seem most rude,
For that informs me how I am subdu'd.
Gods, you're unjust to tyrannize o'er me,
When thousands fitter for't than I go free.
[Ex.

FALATIUS - Why, what the Devil has possest Alcander?

OLINDA - How like you this, Aminta?

AMINTA - Better and better, he's a wondrous man.

[Exeunt Am. and Oli.

FALATIUS - 'Tis the most unjanty humour that ever I saw;
Ay, ay, he is my Rival,
No marvel an he look'd so big upon me;
He is damnable valiant, and as jealous as
He is valiant; how shall I behave my
Self to him, and these too idle humours of his
I cannot yet determine; the comfort is,
He knows I am a Coward whatever face I set upon it.
Well, I must either resolve never to provoke
His Jealousy, or be able to rencounter his
Other fury, his Valour; that were a good

Resolve if I be not past all hope.

[Ex.

SCENE III.

Enter Alcippus and Erminia, as in a Bed-Chamber.

ALCIPPUS - But still methinks, Erminia, you are sad,
A heaviness appears in those fair Eyes,
As if your Soul were agitating something
Contrary to the pleasure of this night.

ERMINIA - You ought in Justice, Sir, t'excuse me here,
Prisoners when first committed are less gay,
Than when they're us'd to Fetters every day,
But yet in time they will more easy grow.

ALCIPPUS - You strangely bless me in but saying so.

ERMINIA - Alcippus, I've an humble suit to you.

ALCIPPUS - All that I have is so intirely thine,
And such a Captive thou hast made my Will,
Thou needst not be at the expence of wishing
For what thou canst desire that I may grant;
Why are thy Eyes declin'd?

ERMINIA - To satisfy a little modest scruple;
I beg you would permit me, Sir.

ALCIPPUS - To lie alone to night, is it not so, Erminia?

ERMINIA - It is -

ALCIPPUS - That's too severe, yet I will grant it thee?
But why, Erminia, must I grant it thee?

ERMINIA - The Princess, Sir, questions my Power, and says,
I cannot gain so much upon your Goodness.

ALCIPPUS - I could have wish'd some other had oblig'd thee to't.

ERMINIA - You would not blame her if you knew her reason.

ALCIPPUS - Indeed I do not much, for I can guess
She takes the party of the Prince her Brother;
And this is only to delay those Joys,
Which she perhaps believes belong to him.

But that, Erminia, you can best resolve;
And 'tis not kindly done to hide a truth,
The Prince so clearly own'd.

ERMINIA - What did he own?

ALCIPPUS - He said, Erminia, that you were his Wife;
If so, no wonder you refuse my Bed: [She weeps.
The Presence of the King hinder'd my knowledge,
Of what I willingly would learn from you;
Come, ne'er deny a truth that plain appears;
I see Hypocrisy through all your Tears.

ERMINIA - You need not ask me to repeat again,
A Knowledge which, you say, appears so plain:
The Prince his word methinks should credit get,
Which I'll confirm whene'er you call for it:
My heart before you ask't it, was his prize,
And cannot twice become a Sacrifice.

ALCIPPUS - Erminia, is this brave or just in you,
To pay his score of Love with what's my due?
What's your design to treat me in this sort?
Are sacred Vows of Marriage made your sport?
Regard me well, Erminia, what am I?

ERMINIA - One, Sir, with whom, I'm bound to live and die,
And one to whom, by rigorous command,
I gave (without my Heart) my unwilling Hand.

ALCIPPUS - But why, Erminia, did you give it so?

ERMINIA - T'obey a King and cruel Father too.
A Friendship, Sir, I can on you bestow,
But that will hardly into Passion grow;
And 'twill an Act below your Virtue prove,
To force a Heart you know can never love.

ALCIPPUS - Am I the mask to hide your Blushes in,
I the contented Fool to veil your Sin?
Have you already learnt that trick at Court,
Both how to practise and secure your sport?
Brave Mistress of your Art, is this the way,
My Service and my Passion to repay?
Will nothing but a Prince your pleasure fit,
And could you think that I would wink at it?
Recal that Folly, or by all that's good,
I'll free the Soul that wantons in thy Blood.
[He in rage takes her by the arm, shews a dagger.

ERMINIA - I see your Love your Reason has betray'd,

But I'll forgive the Faults which Love has made:
'Tis true, I love, and do confess it too;
Which if a Crime, I might have hid from you;
But such a Passion 'tis as does despise
Whatever Rage you threaten from your Eyes.
Yes, you may disapprove this flame in me,
But cannot hinder what the Gods decree;
Search here this truth; Alas, I cannot fear;
Your Steel shall find a welcome entrance here.

[He holds her still and gazes on her.

ALCIPPUS - Where dost thou think thy ungrateful Soul will go,
Loaded with wrongs to me, should I strike now?

ERMINIA - To some blest place, where Lovers do reside,
Free from the noise of Jealousy and Pride;
Where we shall know no other Power but Love,
And where even thou wilt soft and gentle prove;
So gentle, that if I should meet thee there,
Thou would'st allow, what thou deny'st me here.

ALCIPPUS - Thou hast disarm'd my Rage, and in its room
A world of Shame and softer Passions come,
Such as the first efforts of Love inspir'd,
When by thy charming Eyes my Soul was fir'd.

ERMINIA - I must confess your Fears are seeming just,
But here to free you from the least mistrust,
I swear, whilst I'm your Wife I'll not allow
Birth to a Thought that tends to injuring you.

ALCIPPUS - Not to believe thee, were a sin above
The Injuries I have done thee by my Love.
Ah, my Erminia, might I hope at last
To share the pity of that lovely Breast,
By slow degrees I might approach that Throne,
Where now the blest Philander reigns alone:
Perhaps in time my Passion might redeem
That now too faithful Heart y'ave given to him;
Do but forbear to hear his amorous Tales,
Nor from his moving Eyes learn what he ails:
A Fire that's kindled cannot long survive,
If one add nought to keep the flame alive.

ERMINIA - I will not promise; what I mean to do
My Virtue only shall oblige me to.

ALCIPPUS - But, Madam, what d'you mean by this reserve?
To what intent does all this Coldness serve?
Is there no pity to my Sufferings due?

And will you still my Languishments renew?
Come, come, recal what you have rashly said;
And own to morrow that thou art no Maid:
Thy Blushes do betray thy willingness,
And in thy lovely Eyes I read success.

ERMINIA - A double tie obliges me to be
Strict to my Vows, my Love and Amity;
For my own sake the first I'll ne'er decline,
And I would gladly keep the last for thine.

ALCIPPUS - Madam, you strangely do improve my pain,
To give me hopes you must recal again.

ERMINIA - Alcippus, you this language will forbear,
When you shall know how powerful you are;
For whilst you here endeavour to subdue,
The best of Women languishes for you.

ALCIPPUS - Erminia, do not mock my misery,
For though you cannot love, yet pity me;
That you allow my Passion no return,
Is weight enough, you need not add your Scorn,
In this your Cruelty is too severe.

ERMINIA - Alcippus, you mistake me every where.

ALCIPPUS - To whom, Erminia, do I owe this Fate?

ERMINIA - To morrow all her story I'll relate.
Till then the promise I the Princess made,
I beg you would permit might be obey'd.

ALCIPPUS - You, Madam, with so many charms assail,
You need not question but you shall prevail;
Thy power's not lessen'd in thy being mine,
But much augmented in my being thine,
The glory of my chains may raise me more,
But I am still that Slave I was before.

[Exeunt severally.

SCENE IV. Philander's Bed-chamber.

Enter Philander and Alcander. [The Prince half undrest.

PHILANDER - What's a Clock, Alcander?

ALCANDER - 'Tis midnight, Sir, will you not go to bed?

PHILANDER - To bed, Friend; what to do?

ALCANDER - To sleep, Sir, as you were wont to do.

PHILANDER - Sleep, and Erminia have abandon'd me;
I'll never sleep again.

ALCANDER - This is an humour, Sir, you must forsake.

PHILANDER - Never, never, oh Alcander.
Dost know where my Erminia lies to night?

ALCANDER - I guess, Sir.

PHILANDER - Where? Nay, prithee speak,
Indeed I shall not be offended at it.

ALCANDER - I know not why you should, Sir;
She's where she ought, abed with young Alcippus.

PHILANDER - Thou speak'st thy real Thoughts.

ALCANDER - Why should your Highness doubt it?

PHILANDER - By Heaven, there is no faith in Woman-kind;
Alcander, dost thou know an honest Woman?

ALCANDER - Many, Sir.

PHILANDER - I do not think it, 'tis impossible;
Erminia, if it could have been, were she,
But she has broke her Vows, which I held sacred,
And plays the wanton in another's arms.

ALCANDER - Sir, do you think it just to wrong her so?

PHILANDER - Oh, would thou couldst persuade me that I did so.
Thou know'st the Oaths and Vows she made to me,
Never to marry other than my self,
And you, Alcander, wrought me to believe them.
But now her Vows to marry none but me,
Are given to Alcippus, and in his bosom breath'd,
With balmy whispers, whilst the ravisht Youth
For every syllable returns a kiss,
And in the height of all his extasy,
Philander's dispossess'd and quite forgotten.
Ah, charming Maid, is this your Love to me?
Yet now thou art no Maid, nor lov'st not me,
And I the fool to let thee know my weakness.

ALCANDER - Why do you thus proceed to vex your self?
To question what you list, and answer what you please?
Sir, this is not the way to be at ease.

PHILANDER - Ah, dear Alcander, what would'st have me do?

ALCANDER - Do that which may preserve you;
Do that which every Man in love would do;
Make it your business to possess the object.

PHILANDER - What meanest thou, is she not married?

ALCANDER - What then? she'as all about her that she had,
Of Youth and Beauty she is Mistress still,
And may dispose it how and where she will.

PHILANDER - Pray Heaven I do not think too well of thee:
What means all this discourse, art thou honest?

ALCANDER - As most Men of my Age.

PHILANDER - And wouldst thou counsel me to such a Sin?
For I do understand thee.

ALCANDER - I know not what you term so.

PHILANDER - I never thought thou'dst been so great a Villain,
To urge me to a crime would damn us all;
Why dost thou smile, hast thou done well in this?

ALCANDER - I thought so, or I'ad kept it to my self.
Sir, e'er you grow in rage at what I've said,
Do you think I love you, or believe my life
Were to be valued more than your repose?
You seem to think it is not.

PHILANDER - Possibly I may.

ALCANDER - The sin of what I have propos'd to you
You only seem to hate: Sir, is it so?
If such religious thoughts about you dwell,
Why is it that you thus perplex your self?
Self-murder sure is much the greater sin.
Erminia too you say has broke her Vows,
She that will swear and lye, will do the rest.
And of these evils, this I think the least;
And as for me, I never thought it sin.

PHILANDER - And canst thou have so poor a thought of her?

ALCANDER - I hope you'll find her, Sir, as willing to't

As I am to suppose it; nay, believe't,
She'll look upon't as want of Love and Courage
Should you not now attempt it;
You know, Sir, there's no other remedy,
Take no denial, but the Game pursue,
For what she will refuse, she wishes you.

PHILANDER - With such pretensions, she may angry grow.

ALCANDER - I never heard of any that were so,
For though the will to do't, and power they want,
They love to hear of what they cannot grant.

PHILANDER - No more,
Is this your duty to your Prince, Alcander?
You were not wont to counsel thus amiss,
'Tis either Disrespect or some Design;
I could be wondrous angry with thee now,
But that my Grief has such possession here,
'Twill make no room for Rage.

ALCANDER - I cannot, Sir, repent of what I've said,
Since all the errors which I have committed
Are what my passion to your interest led me to,
But yet I beg your Highness would recal
That sense which would persuade you 'tis unjust.

PHILANDER - Name it no more, and I'll forgive it thee.

ALCANDER - I can obey you, Sir.

PHILANDER - What shall we do to night, I cannot sleep.

ALCANDER - I'm good at watching, and doing any thing.

PHILANDER - We'll serenade the Ladies and the Bride.
The first we may disturb, but she I fear
Keeps watch with me to night, though not like me.

Enter a Page of the Prince's.

PHILANDER - How now, Boy,
Is the Musick ready which I spoke for?

PAGE - They wait your Highness's command.

PHILANDER - Bid them prepare, I'm coming.   [Ex. Page -
Soft touches may allay the Discords here,
And sweeten, though not lessen my Despair.

[Exeunt.

SCENE V. The Court Gallery.

Enter Pisaro alone.

PISARO - Ha! who's that? a Lover, on my life,
This amorous malady reigns every where;
Nor can my Sister be an ignorant
Of what I saw this night in Galatea:
I'll question her, Sister, Aminta, Sister.
[Calls as at her Lodgings.

Enter Lysette.

Lysette - Who calls my Lady?

PISARO - Where's my Sister?

Lysette - I cry your Lordship's mercy;
My Lady lies not in her Lodgings to night;
The Princess sent for her,
Her Highness is not well.
[She goes in.

PISARO - I do believe it, good night, Lysette.

Enter a Page.

Who's there?

PAGE - Your Lordship's Page.

PISARO - Where hast thou been? I wanted thee but now.

PAGE - I fell asleep i'th' Lobby, Sir, and had not waken'd
Yet, but for the Musick which plays at the Lodgings
Of my Lady Erminia.

PISARO - Curse on them; will they not allow him nights to himself;
'tis hard.
This night I'm wiser grown by observation,
My Love and Friendship taught me jealousy,
Which like a cunning Spy brought in intelligence
From every eye less wary than its own;
They told me that the charming Galatea,
In whom all power remains,
Is yet too feeble to encounter Love;
I find she has receiv'd the wanton God,
Maugre my fond opinion of her Soul.

And 'tis my Friend too that's become my Rival.
I saw her lovely Eyes still turn on him,
As Flowers to th'Sun: and when he turn'd away
Like those she bow'd her charming head again.
On th'other side the Prince with dying looks
Each motion watch'd of fair Erminia's eyes,
Which she return'd as greedily again,
And if one glance t' Alcippus she directed,
He'd stare as if he meant to cut his throat for't.

Well, Friend, thou hast a sure defence of me,
My Love is yet below my Amity.

[Ex.

SCENE VI. Draws off, Discovers Philander and Alcander with Musick at the Chamber-door of Erminia; to them Pisaro, who Listens whilst the Song is Sung.

The Song for the Page to sing at Erminia's Chamber-door.

Amintas that true-hearted Swain
Upon a River's bank was laid,
Where to the pitying streams he did complain
Of Sylvia that false charming Maid,
But she was still regardless of his pain:
Oh faithless Sylvia! would he cry,
And what he said the Echoes would reply.
Be kind or else I die, E. I die.
Be kind or else I die, E. I die.

A shower of tears his eyes let fall,
Which in the River made impress,
Then sigh'd, and Sylvia false again would call,
A cruel faithless Shepherdess.
Is Love with you become a criminal?
Ah lay aside this needless scorn,
Allow your poor Adorer some return,
Consider how I burn, E. I burn.
Consider, &c.

Those Smiles and Kisses which you give.
Remember, Sylvia, are my due;
And all the Joys my Rival does receive
He ravishes from me, not you.
Ah Sylvia, can I live and this believe?
Insensibles are touched to see
My languishments, and seem to pity me.
Which I demand of thee, E. of thee,
Which I demand, &c.

PISARO - What's all this?

PHILANDER - Who's there?

PISARO - A Man, a Friend to the General.

PHILANDER - Then thou'rt an Enemy to all good Men.
Does the ungrateful Wretch hide his own head,
And send his Spies abroad?

PISARO - He is too great to fear, and needs them not:
And him thou termest so, scorns the Office too.

PHILANDER - What makest thou here then, when the whole World's asleep?
Be gone, there lies thy way, where'er thy business be.

PISARO - It lies as free for thee, and here's my business.

PHILANDER - Thou lyest, rude man.

PISARO - Why, what art thou darest tell me so i'th' dark?
Day had betray'd thy blushes for this Boldness.

PHILANDER - Tell me who 'tis that dares capitulate?

PISARO - One that dares make it good.

PHILANDER - Draw then, and keep thy word.

ALCANDER - Stand by, and let me do that duty, Sir.
[He steps between them, they fight, Pisaro falls.
Here's thy reward, whoe'er thou art.

PHILANDER - Hast thou no hurt?

ALCANDER - I think not much, yet somewhere 'tis I bleed.

PISARO - What a dull beast am I!

[Exeunt Prince and Alcan.

Enter Page.

PAGE - My Lord, is't you are fallen?
Help, Murder! Murder!

PISARO - Hold, bawling Dog.

Enter Alcippus in a Night-gown, with a Sword
in his hand, a Page with Lights.

ALCIPPUS - 'Twas hereabouts, who's this, Pisaro wounded?
[He looks up.
How cam'st thou thus? Come up into my Arms.

PISARO - 'Twas Jealousy, Alcippus, that wild Monster,
Who never leaves us till he has thus betray'd us.
Pox on't, I am asham'd to look upon thee.
I have disturb'd you to no purpose, Sir.
I am not wounded, go to bed again.

ALCANDER - I'll see thee to thy Lodgings first, Pisaro.

PISARO - 'Twill be unkind both to your self and me.

[Exeunt.

SCENE VII. The Court Gallery.

Enter Philander and Alcander with a Light.

ALCANDER - He's gone, whoe'er he be.

PHILANDER - It could not be Alcippus.

ALCANDER - I rather fear Pisaro,
But we soon enough shall know: Who's this?

Enter Erminia in her Night-gown, and Isillia with Lights.

ERMINIA - Methought I heard Alcippus and the Prince
Before the cry of Murder.
I die if those two Rivals have encounter'd.

PHILANDER - Ah, Madam, cease that fear, they both are safe
From all but from the Wounds which you have given them.

ERMINIA - Oh Gods, what make you here! and where's Alcippus?

PHILANDER - Where I had been had Heaven been bountiful.

ERMINIA - Alas, Sir, what do you mean? what have you done?
And where have you bestow'd him?

PHILANDER - Why all this high concern, Erminia?
Has he so reconcil'd you to him since I saw you last?
This is not kind to me.

ERMINIA - Oh, tell me not of kindness, where's Alcippus?

ALCANDER - Madam, of whom do you demand Alcippus?
Neither of us have seen him.

PHILANDER - Go, you are a Woman, a vain peevish Creature.

ERMINIA - Sir, 'tis but just you should excuse my Fear,
Alcippus is my Husband, and his Safety
Ought to become my care.

PHILANDER - How, Erminia!
Can you so soon yield up my right to him,
And not blush whilst you own your Perjury?

ERMINIA - Now, Sir, you are much to blame;
I could have borne the rest, but this concerns me:
I fear I have but too well kept my Vows with you,
Since you are grown but to suspect I have not.

PHILANDER - Pardon me, Dear, the errors of my Passion;
It was a Sin so natural,
That even thy unkindly taking it
Approach'd too near it, not to gain my Pardon;
But tell me why you askt me for Alcippus?

ERMINIA - Sir, e'er I could dispose my Eyes to sleep,
I heard the Musick at my Chamber-door,
And such a Song as could be none but yours;
But that was finish'd in a noise less pleasant,
In that of Swords and Quarrel;
And amongst which,
I thought I heard yours and Alcippus' Voice:
(For I have kept my word, and lay not with him)
This brought me hither; but if I mistook,
Once more I beg your pardon.

PHILANDER - Thou hast restor'd me to a world of Joys,
By what thou now hast said.

Enter Alcippus, his Sword in his Hand, a
Page with Light, he stands a while.

ALCIPPUS - Erminia! and the Prince! embracing too!
I dream, and know she could not be thus base,
Thus false and loose
But here I am inform'd it is no Vision;
This was design'd before, I find it now.
[Lays his hand on his heart.

ERMINIA - Alcippus, oh my fears!
[Goes to them, takes her by the hand.

ALCIPPUS - Yes, Madam,
Too soon arriv'd for his and your repose.

PHILANDER - Alcippus, touch her not.

ALCIPPUS - Not touch her! by Heaven, I will,
And who shall hinder me?
Who is't dares say I shall not touch my Wife?

PHILANDER - Villain, thou ly'st.

ALCIPPUS - That y'are my Prince shall not defend you here.
Draw, Sir, for I have laid respect aside.

[Strikes, they fight a little, Alcippus is
wounded, Alcander supports him.

ERMINIA - Oh Gods, what mean you? hold, Philander, hold.

PHILANDER - Life of my Soul, retire,
I cannot hear that Voice and disobey;
And you must needs esteem him at low rates,
Who sells thee and his Honour for a Tear.

ERMINIA - Upon my knees I beg to be obey'd,   [She kneels.
But if I must not, here discharge your Anger.

PHILANDER - You are too great a Tyrant where you may.

[Exeunt Erminia and Alcippus.

PHILANDER - Stay, shall I let her go? shall her Commands,
Though they have power to take my Life away,
Have force to suffer me to injure her?
Shall she be made a prey, and I permit it,
Who only have the interest to forbid it?
No, let me be accurst then.
[Offers to follow.

ALCANDER - What mean you, Sir?

PHILANDER - Force the bold Ravisher to resign my Right.
Alcander, is not she my Wife, and I his Prince?

ALCANDER - 'Tis true, Sir:
And y'ave both power and justice on your side;
And there are times to exercise 'em both.

PHILANDER - Fitter than this, Alcander?

ALCANDER - This night Erminia's Promise may repose you;
To morrow is your own -
Till then I beg you'd think your interest safe.

Phi. Alcander, thou hast peace about thee, and canst judge
Better than I, 'twixt what is just and fit.
[Puts up his Sword.
I hitherto believ'd my Flame was guided
By perfect Reason: so we often find
Vessels conducted by a peaceful Wind,
And meet no opposition in their way,
Cut a safe passage through the flattering Sea:
But when a Storm the bounding Vessel throws,
It does each way with equal rage oppose;
For when the Seas are mad, could that be calm
Like me, it wou'd be ruin'd in the Storm.

[Exeunt.

ACT III.

SCENE I. The Apartments of Alcippus.

Enter Alcippus and Pisaro.

PISARO - 'Tis much, my Lord, you'll not be satisfy'd.

ALCIPPUS - Friendship's too near a-kin to Love, Pisaro,
To leave me any Peace, whilst in your Eyes
I read Reserves, which 'tis not kind to hide;
Come, prithee tell me what the quarrel was,
And who 'twas with; thou shalt, my dear Pisaro.

PISARO - Nay, now you urge me to impossibility:
Good faith, I cannot tell, but guess the Prince.

ALCIPPUS - 'Tis true, Pisaro, 'twas indeed the Prince.
But what was th'occasion?

PISARO - He call'd me Spy, and I return'd th'affront,
But took no notice that he was my Prince:
It was a Folly I repented of;
But 'twas in a damn'd melancholy Mood.

ALCIPPUS - Was it a going in or coming out?

PISARO - From whence?

Alcip. Erminia's Chamber; prithee let me know,

For I have fears that take away my sleep,
Fears that will make me mad, stark mad, Pisaro.

PISARO - You do not well to fear without a cause.

ALCIPPUS - O Friend, I saw what thou canst ne'er conceive;
Last night I saw it when I came from thee:
And if thou go'st about t'impose upon me,
I'll cast thee from my Soul. Come out with it,
I see thy breast heave with a generous ardour,
As if it scorn'd to harbour a reserve,
Which stood not with its Amity to me.
Could I but know my Fate, I could despise it:
But when 'tis clad in Robes of Innocence,
The Devil cannot 'scape it: Something
Was done last night that gnaws my heart-strings;
And many things the Princess too let fall,
Which, Gods! I know not how to put together.
And prithee be not thou a Ridler too:
But if thou knew'st of ought that may concern me,
Make me as wise as thou art.

PISARO - Sir, you are of so strange a jealous Humour,
And I so strangely jealous of your Honour,
That 'twixt us both we may make work enough;
But on my Soul I know no wrong you have.

ALCIPPUS - I must believe thee, yet methinks thy Face
Has put on an unwonted gravity.

PISARO - That, Alcippus, you'll not wonder at,
When you shall know you are my Rival.

ALCIPPUS - Nay, why shouldst thou delay me thus with stories?
This shall not put me off.

PISARO - Sir, I'm in earnest, you have gain'd that Heart,
For which I have receiv'd so many wounds;
Venturing for Trophies where none durst appear,
To gain at my Return one single smile,
Or that she would submit to hear my story:
And when sh'has said, 'twas bravely done, Pisaro,
I thought the Glory recompens'd the Toil;
And sacrificed my Laurels at her feet,
Like those who pay their first-fruits to the Gods,
To beg a blessing on the following Crop:
And never made her other signs of Love,
Nor knew I that I had that easy flame,
Till by her Eyes I found that she was mortal,
And could love too, and that my Friend is you.

ALCIPPUS - Thou hast amaz'd me, prithee speak more clearly.

PISARO - My Lord, the Princess has a passion for you,
Have I not reason now to be your Enemy?

ALCIPPUS - Not till I make returns:
But now I'm past redemption miserable.
'Twas she Erminia told me dy'd for me;
And I believ'd it but a slight of hers,
To put me from my Courtship.

PISARO - No, 'twas a fatal Truth:
Alcippus, hadst thou seen her, whilst the Priest
Was giving thee to fair Erminia,
What languishment appear'd upon her Eyes,
Which never were remov'd from thy lov'd Face,
Through which her melting Soul in drops distill'd,
As if she meant to wash away thy Sin,
In giving up that Right belong'd to her,
Thou hadst without my aid found out this truth:
A sweet composure dwelt upon her looks,
Like Infants who are smiling whilst they die;
Nor knew she that she wept, so unconcern'd
And freely did her Soul a passage find;
Whilst I transported had almost forgot
The Reverence due t'her sacred self and Place,
And every moment ready was to kneel,
And with my lips gather the precious drops,
And rob the Holy Temple of a Relick,
Fit only there t'inhabit.

ALCIPPUS - I never thought thou'dst had this Softness in thee.
How cam'st thou, Friend, to hide all this from me?

PISARO - My Lord, I knew not that I was a Lover;
I felt no flame, but a religious Ardour,
That did inspire my Soul with adoration;
And so remote I was from ought but such,
I knew not Hope, nor what it was to wish
For other blessings than to gaze upon her:
Like Heaven I thought she was to be possess'd,
Where carnal Thoughts can no admittance find;
And had I not perceiv'd her Love to you,
I had not known the nature of my flame:
But then I found it out by Jealousy,
And what I took for a Seraphick motion,
I now decline as criminal and earthly.

ALCIPPUS - When she can love to a discovery,
It shows her Passion eminent and high;
But I am married to a Maid that hates me:

What help for that, Pisaro?
And thou hast something too to say of her,
What was't? for now thou hast undone me quite.

PISARO - I have nought to say to her dishonour, Sir,
But something may be done may give you cause
To stand upon your Guard;
And if your Rage do not the mastery get,
I cannot doubt but what you'll be happy yet.

ALCIPPUS - Without Erminia that can hardly be,
And yet I find a certain shame within
That will not suffer me to see the Princess;
I have a kind of War within my Soul,
My Love against my Glory and my Honour;
And I could wish, alas, I know not what:
Prithee instruct me.

PISARO - Sir, take a resolution to be calm,
And not like Men in love abandon Reason.
You may observe the actions of these Lovers,
But be not passionate whate'er you find;
That headstrong Devil will undo us all;
If you'll be happy, quit its company.

ALCIPPUS - I fain would take thy counsel   [Pauses.

PISARO - Come, clear up, my Lord, and do not hang the head
Like Flowers in storms; the Sun will shine again.
Set Galatea's Charms before your Eyes,
Think of the Glory to divide a Kingdom;
And do not waste your noble Youth and Time
Upon a peevish Heart you cannot gain.
This day you must to th'Camp, and in your absence
I'll take upon me what I scorn'd last night,
The Office of a Spy
Believe me, Sir, for by the Gods I swear,
I never wish'd the glory of a Conquest
With half that zeal as to compose these differences.

ALCIPPUS - I do believe thee, and will tell thee something
That past between the Prince and I last night;
And then thou wilt conclude me truly miserable.

[Exeunt.

SCENE II. The Palace.

Enter Falatius, Labree, as passing by they meet Cleontius.

CLEONTIUS - Your Servant, my Lord.
So coldly, stay your reason, Sir.

[Falatius puts off his Hat a little, and passes on.

FALATIUS - How mean you, Sir?

CLEONTIUS - Do you not know me?

FALATIUS - Yes, I have seen you, and think you are Cleontius,
A Servant of the Prince's; wert i'th' Campania too,
If I mistake not.

CLEONTIUS - Can you recal me by no better instances?

FALATIUS - What need of any, pray?

CLEONTIUS - I am a Gentleman.

FALATIUS - Ha, Labree, what means he now?
By Jove, I do not question it, Cleontius:
What need this odd Punctilio?
I call thee to no account.

CLEONTIUS - That's more than I can say to you, Sir.

FALATIUS - I'll excuse you for that.

CLEONTIUS - But shall not need, Sir; stay, I have a Sister.

FALATIUS - Oh, the Devil, now he begins.

CLEONTIUS - A handsome Sister too, or you deceiv'd her.

LABREE - Bear up, Sir, be not huft.   [Aside.

FALATIUS - It may be so, but is she kind, Cleontius?
[Fal. bears up.

CLEONTIUS - What mean you by that word?

LABREE - Again, Sir, here's two to one.   [Aside.

FALATIUS - Will she do reason, or so? you understand me.

CLEONTIUS - I understand that thou'rt an impudent fellow,
Whom I must cudgel into better manners.

FALATIUS - Pox on't, who bears up now, Labree?

CLEONTIUS - Beat thee till thou confess thou art an Ass,
And on thy knees confess it to Isillia,
Who after that shall scorn thee.

LABREE - Railly with him, Sir, 'tis your only way, and put it
Off with a jest; for he's in fury, but dares not
Strike i'th' Court.

FALATIUS - But must you needs do this, needs fight, Cleontius?

CLEONTIUS - Yes, by all means, I find my self inclin'd to't.

FALATIUS - You shall have your desire, Sir, farewel.

CLEONTIUS - When, and where?

FALATIUS - Faith, very suddenly, for I think it will not be
Hard to find men of your trade,
Men that will fight as long as you can do,
And Men that love it much better than I,
Men that are poor and damn'd, fine desperate Rogues,
Rascals that for a Pattacoon a Man
Will fight their Fathers,
And kiss their Mothers into peace again:
Such, Sir, I think will fit you.

CLEONTIUS - Abusive Coward, hast thou no sense of honour?

FALATIUS - Sense of honour! ha, ha, ha, poor Cleontius.

Enter Aminta and Olinda.

AMINTA - How now, Servant, why so jovial?

FALATIUS - I was laughing, Madam at -

CLEONTIUS - At what, thou thing of nothing -

AMINTA - Cousin Cleontius, you are angry.

CLEONTIUS - Madam, it is unjustly then, for Fools
Should rather move the Spleen to Mirth than Anger.

AMINTA - You've too much wit to take ought ill from him:
Let's know your quarrel.

FALATIUS - By Jove, Labree, I am undone again.

CLEONTIUS - Madam, it was about -

FALATIUS - Hold, dear Cleontius, hold, and I'll do any thing. [Aside.

CLEONTIUS - Just nothing -

FALATIUS - He was a little too familiar with me.

CLEONTIUS - Madam, my Sister Isillia -

FALATIUS - A curse, he will out with it
[Aside, pulls him by the Arm.

CLEONTIUS - Confess she is your Mistress.   [Aside.

FALATIUS - I call my Mistress, Madam.

AMINTA - My Cousin Isillia your Mistress!
Upon my word, you are a happy Man.

FALATIUS - By Jove, if she be your Cousin, Madam,
I love her much the better for't.

AMINTA - I am beholding to you,
But then it seems I have lost a Lover of you.

CLEONTIUS - Confess she has, or I'll so handle you.

[Ex. Labree.

FALATIUS - That's too much, Cleontius, but I will,
By Jove, Madam, I must not have a Mistress that
Has more Wit than my self, they ever require
More than a Man's able to give them.

OLINDA - Is this your way of Courtship to Isillia?

[Ex. Cleontius.

FALATIUS - By Jove, Ladies, you get no more of that from me,
'Tis that has spoiled you all; I find Alcander can
Do more with a dumb show, than I with all my
Applications and Address.

OLINDA - Why, my Brother can speak.

FALATIUS - Yes, if any body durst hear him; by Jove, if you
Be not kind to him, he'll hector you all; I'll get
The way on't too, 'tis the most prosperous one; I see no
Other reason you have to love Alcander
Better than I.

AMINTA - Why should you think I do?

FALATIUS - Devil, I see't well enough by your continual
Quarrels with him.

AMINTA - Is that so certain a proof?

FALATIUS - Ever while you live, you treat me too
Well ever to hope.

Enter Alcander, kneels, offers his Sword to Aminta.

What new Masquerade's this? by Jove, Alcander
Has more tricks than a dancing Bear.

AMINTA - What mean you by this present?

ALCANDER - Kill me.

AMINTA - What have you done to merit it?

ALCANDER - Do not ask, but do't.

AMINTA - I'll have a reason first.

ALCANDER - I think I've kill'd Pisaro.

AMINTA - My Brother dead!
[She falls into the arms of Oli.

FALATIUS - Madam, look up, 'tis I that call.

AMINTA - I care not who thou beest, but if a Man,
Revenge me on Alcander.
[She goes out with Oli.

FALATIUS - By Jove, she has mistook her Man,
This 'tis to be a Lover now:
A Man's never out of one broil or other;
But I have more Wit than Aminta this bout.   [Offers to go.

ALCANDER - Come back and do your duty e'er you go.   [Pulls him.

FALATIUS - I owe you much, Alcander.

ALCANDER - Amimta said you should revenge her on me.

FALATIUS - Her Word's not Law I hope.

ALCANDER - And I'll obey.

FALATIUS - That may do much indeed.
[Fal. answers with great signs of fear.

ALCANDER - This, if thou wert a Man, she bad thee do,
Why dost thou shake?

FALATIUS - No, no, Sir, I am not the man she meant.

ALCANDER - No matter, thou wilt serve as well.
A Lover! and canst disobey thy Mistress?

FALATIUS - I do disown her, since she is so wicked
To bid me kill my Friend.
Why, thou'rt my Friend, Alcander.

ALCANDER - I'll forgive thee that.

FALATIUS - So will not his Majesty: I may be hang'd for't.

ALCANDER - Thou should'st be damn'd e'er disobey thy Mistress.

FALATIUS - These be degrees of Love I am not yet arriv'd at;
When I am, I shall be as ready to be damn'd
In honour as any Lover of you all.

ALCANDER - Ounds, Sir, d'ye railly with me?

FALATIUS - Your pardon, sweet Alcander, I protest I am
Not in so gay an humour.

ALCANDER - Farewell, I had forgot my self.
[Exit.

FALATIUS - Stark mad, by Jove, yet it may be not, for
Alcander has many unaccountable humours.
Well, if this be agreeable to Aminta, she's e'en as mad
As he, and 'twere great pity to part them.

Enter Pisaro, Aminta, and Olinda.

AMINTA - Well, have you kill'd him?

FALATIUS - Some wiser than some, Madam.
My Lord, what, alive?
[Sees Pisaro, runs to him, and embraces him.

PISARO - Worth two dead men, you see.

FALATIUS - That's more than I could have said within
This half hour. Alcander's very Orlando, by Jove, and gone
To seek out one that's madder yet than himself
That will kill him.

AMINTA - Oh, dear Falatius, run and fetch him back.

FALATIUS - Madam, I have so lately 'scap'd a scouring,
That I wish you would take it for a mark
Of my Passion to disobey you;
For he is in a damn'd humour.

AMINTA - He's out of it by this, I warrant you;
But do not tell him that Pisaro lives.

FALATIUS - That's as I shall find occasion.
[Exit Falatius.

PISARO - Alcander is a worthy Youth and brave,
I wish you would esteem him so;
'Tis true, there's now some difference between us,
Our Interests are dispos'd to several ways,
But Time and Management will join us all:
I'll leave you; but prithee make it thy business
To get my Pardon for last night's rudeness.

AMINTA - I shall not fail.

[Exit Pisaro.

Re-enter Falatius, with Alcander melancholy.

FALATIUS - Here, Madam, here he is.

AMINTA - Tell me, Alcander, why you treat me thus?
You say you love me, if I could believe you.

ALCANDER - Believe a Man! away, you have no wit,
I'll say as much to every pretty Woman.

AMINTA - But I have given you no cause to wrong me.

ALCANDER - That was my Fate, not Fault, I knew him not:
But yet to make up my offence to you,
I offer you my life; for I'm undone,
If any faults of mine should make you sad.

AMINTA - Here, take your Sword again, my Brother's well.
[She gives him his Sword again.

FALATIUS - Yes, by Jove, as I am: you had been finely serv'd,
If I had kill'd you now.

AMINTA - What, sorry for the news? ha, ha, ha.

ALCANDER - No, sorry y'are a Woman, a mere Woman.

AMINTA - Why, did you ever take me for a Man? ha, ha.

ALCANDER - Thy Soul, I thought, was all so; but I see
You have your weakness, can dissemble too;
I would have sworn that Sorrow in your face
Had been a real one:
Nay, you can die in jest, you can, false Woman:
I hate thy Sex for this.

FALATIUS - By Jove, there is no truth in them, that's flat.
[She looks sad.

ALCANDER - Why that repentant look? what new design?
Come, now a tear or two to second that,
And I am soft again, a very Ass.
But yet that Look would call a Saint from th'Altar,
And make him quite forget his Ceremony,
Or take thee for his Deity:
But yet thou hast a very Hell within,
Which those bewitching Eyes draw Souls into.

FALATIUS - Here's he that fits you, Ladies.

AMINTA - Nay, now y'are too unjust, and I will leave you.

ALCANDER - Ah, do not go, I know not by what Magick,
[Holds her.
But as you move, my Soul yields that way too.

FALATIUS - The truth on't is, she has a strong magnetick Power, that I find.

ALCANDER - But I would have none find it but my self,
No Soul but mine shall sympathize with hers.

FALATIUS - Nay, that you cannot help.

ALCANDER - Yes, but I can, and take it from thee, if I thought it did so.

OLINDA - No quarrels here, I pray.

FALATIUS - Madam, I owe a Reverence to the Place.

ALCANDER - I'll scarce allow thee that;
Madam, I'll leave you to your Lover.

AMINTA - I hate thee but for saying so.

ALCANDER - Quit him then.

AMINTA - So I can and thee too.   [Offers to go out.

ALCANDER - The Devil take me if you escape me so.   [Goes after her.

FALATIUS - And I'll not be out-done in importunity.

[Goes after.

SCENE III. Galatea's Apartments.

Enter Galatea and Erminia.

ERMINIA - And 'tis an act below my Quality,
Which, Madam, will not suffer me to fly.

GALATEA - Erminia, e'er you boast of what you are,
Since you're so high I'll tell you what you were:
Your Father was our General 'tis true,
That Title justly to his Sword was due;
'Twas nobly gain'd, and worth his Blood and Toils,
Had he been satisfied with noble Spoils:
But with that single honour not content,
He needs must undermine the Government;
And 'cause h'ad gain'd the Army to his side,
Believ'd his Treason must be justify'd.
For this (and justly) he was banished;
Where whilst a low and unknown life he led,
Far from the hope and glory of a Throne,
In a poor humble Cottage you were born;
Your early Beauty did it self display,
Nor could no more conceal it self than Day:
Your Eyes did first Philander's Soul inspire,
And Fortune too conform'd her to his fire.
That made your Father greater than before,
And what he justly lost that did restore.
'Twas that which first thy Beauty did disclose,
Which else had wither'd like an unseen Rose;
'Twas that which brought thee to the Court, and there
Dispos'd thee next my self, i'th' highest Sphere:
Alas, obscurely else thou'dst liv'd and died,
Not knowing thy own Charms, nor yet this Pride.

ERMINIA - Madam, in this your Bounty is severe,
Be pleas'd to spare that repetition here.
I hope no Action of my Life should be
So rude to charge your Generosity:
But, Madam, do you think it just to pay
Your great Obligements by so false a way?
Alcippus' Passion merits some return,
And should that prove but an ingrateful scorn?

Alas, I am his Wife; to disobey,
My Fame as well as Duty I betray.

GALATEA - Perfidious Maid, I might have thought thou'dst prove
False to thy Prince, and Rival in my Love.
I thought too justly he that conquer'd me
Had a sufficient power to captive thee;
Thou'st now reveng'd thy Father's shame and thine,
In taking thus Philander's Life and mine.

[Ermina weeps.

ERMINIA - Ah, Madam, that you would believe my tears,
Or from my Vows but satisfy your Fears.
By all the Gods, Alcippus I do hate,
And would do any thing to change my fate;
Ought that were just and noble I dare do.

GALATEA - Enough, Erminia, I must credit you,
And will no other proof of it require,
But that you'll now submit to my desire;
Indeed, Erminia, you must grant my suit,
Where Love and Honour calls, make no dispute.
Pity a Youth that never lov'd before,
Remember 'tis a Prince that does adore;
Who offers up a Heart that never found
It could receive, till from your Eyes, a wound.

ERMINIA - To your command should I submit to yield,
Where could I from Alcippus be conceal'd?
What could defend me from his jealous Rage?

GALATEA - Trust me, Erminia, I'll for that engage.

ERMINIA - And then my Honour by that flight's o'erthrown.

GALATEA - That being Philander's, he'll preserve his own;
And that, Erminia, sure you'll ne'er distrust.

ERMINIA - Ah, Madam, give me leave to fear the worst.

Enter Aminta.

AMINTA - Madam, Alcippus waits for your Commands,
He's going to the Camp.

GALATEA - Admit him.

Enter Alcippus and Pisaro.

Gal. Alcippus, 'tis too soon to leave Erminia.

ALCIPPUS - I wish she thought so, Madam,
Or could believe with what regret I do so;
She then would think the fault were much too small
For such a Penance as my Soul must suffer.

AMINTA - No matter, Sir, you have the Year before you.

ALCIPPUS - Yes, Madam, so has every Galley Slave,
That knows his Toil, but not his Recompence:
To morrow I expect no more content,
Than this uneasy Day afforded me;
And all before me is but one grand piece
Of endless Grief and Madness:
You, Madam, taught Erminia to be cruel,
A Vice without your aid she could have learnt;
And now to exercise that new taught Art,
She tries the whole experience on my Heart.

GALATEA - If she do so, she learnt it not of me,
I love, and therefore know no Cruelty:
Such outrage cannot well with Love reside,
Which only is the mean effect of Pride:
I merit better thoughts from you, Alcippus.

ALCIPPUS - Pardon me, Madam, if my Passion stray
Beyond the limits of my high respect;   [He kneels.
'Tis a rude gust, and merits your reproaches:
But yet the saucy Flame can ne'er controul
That Adoration which I owe my Princess:
That, with Religion, took possession here,
And in my Prayers I mix with you the Deities.

GALATEA - I'ad rather you should treat me as a Mortal,
Rise and begin to do so.

[He rises and bows.

ALCIPPUS - Now, Madam, what must I expect from you?

ERMINIA - Alcippus, all that's to your Virtue due.

ALCIPPUS - In that but common Justice you allow.

ERMINIA - That Justice, Sir, is all I can bestow.

ALCIPPUS - In justice then you ought to me resign,
That which the Holy Priest intitled mine;
Yet that, without your Heart, I do despise,
For uncompell'd I'd have that sacrifice:
Come ease me of that Pain that presses here,

Give me but Hope that may secure my Fear,
I'm not asham'd to own my Soul possest
With Jealousy, that takes away my rest.
Tell me you'll love, or that my Suit is vain,
Do any thing to ease me of my pain.
Gods, Madam, why d'ye keep me in suspence?
This cannot be the effects of Innocence;
By Heaven, I'll know the cause, where e'er it lies,
Nor shall you fool me with your feign'd disguise.

PISARO - You do forget your promise, and this Presence.
[Aside to Alcip.

ALCIPPUS - 'Twas kindly urg'd, prithee be near me still,
And tell me of the faults that look unmanly.

GALATEA - Dear, if thou lov'st me, flatter him a little.
[To Ermina aside.

ERMINIA - 'Tis hard to do, yet I will try it, Madam.

GALATEA - I'll leave you, that you may the better do so.
I hope, Alcippus, you'll revisit us
With Lover's speed:
And whatsoever treatment now you find,
At your return you'll find us much more kind.
[He bows, she goes out.

ALCIPPUS - Can you forgive the rashness of a Man,
That knows no other Laws but those of Passion?

ERMINIA - You are unkind to think I do not, Sir;
Yes, and am grown so softned by my pity,
That I'm afraid I shall neglect my Vows,
And to return your Passion, grow ingrate.

ALCIPPUS - A few more syllables express'd like these,
Will raise my Soul up to the worst extreme,
And give me with your Scorn an equal torment.

ERMINIA - See what power your language has upon me.   [Weeps.

ALCIPPUS - Ah, do not weep, a tear or two's enough
For the Completion of your Cruelty,
That when it fail'd to exercise your will,
Sent those more powerful Weapons from your Eyes,
And what by your severity you mist of,
These (but a more obliging way) perform.
Gently, Erminia, pour the Balsam in,
That I may live, and taste the sweets of Love.
Ah, should you still continue, as you are,

Thus wondrous good, thus excellently fair,
I should retain my growing name in War,
And all the Glories I have ventur'd for,
And fight for Crowns to recompense thy Bounty.
This can your Smiles; but when those Beams are clouded,
Alas, I freeze to very Cowardice,
And have not Courage left to kill my self.

ERMINIA - A Fate more glorious does that Life attend,
And does preserve you for a nobler end.

ALCIPPUS - Erminia, do not sooth my easy Heart,
For thou my Fate, and thou my Fortune art;
Whatever other blessings Heaven design,
Without my dear Erminia, I'll decline.
Yet, Madam, let me hope before I go,
In pity that you ought to let me do:
'Tis all you shall allow m'impatient heart.

ERMINIA - That's what against my will I must impart:
But wish it please the Gods, when next we meet,
We might as Friends, and not as Lovers greet.

[Exeunt.

ACT IV.

SCENE I. The Palace.

Enter Galatea and Aminta, met by Philander and Alcander.

PHILANDER - So hasty, Sister!

GALATEA - Brother, I am glad to meet you.
Aminta has some welcome News for you.

AMINTA - My Lord!
Erminia yet is hardly brought to yield;
She wants but some encouragement from you,
That may assist her weakness to subdue,
And 'twas but faintly she deny'd to see you.

PHILANDER - However, I will venture,
She can but chide, and that will soon be past:
A Lover's Anger is not long to last.

AMINTA - Isillia I have won to give you entrance.

PHILANDER - Love furnish me with powerful Arguments:

Direct my Tongue, that my disorder'd Sense
May speak my Passion more than Eloquence.   [Aside.

GALATEA - But is Alcippus gone?

ALCANDER - Madam, an hour since.

PHILANDER - 'Tis well; and Sister,
Whilst I persuade Erminia to this flight,
Make it your business to persuade the King,
Hang on his neck, and kiss his willing cheek:
Tell him how much you love him, and then smile,
And mingle Words with Kisses; 'twill o'ercome him
Thou hast a thousand pretty Flatteries,
Which have appeas'd his highest fits of Passion:
A Song from thee has won him to that rest,
Which neither Toil nor Silence could dispose him to.
Thou know'st thy power, and now or never use it.

GALATEA - 'Twas thither I was going.

PHILANDER - May'st thou be prosperous.

[Exeunt Phi. and Gal. Aminta and Alcander stay.

AMINTA - What now, Alcander?

ALCANDER - As 'twas, Aminta.

AMINTA - How's that?

ALCANDER - Such a distracted Lover as you left me.

AMINTA - Such as I found you too, I fear, Alcander.

ALCANDER - Ah, Madam, do not wrong me so;
Till now I never knew the joys and sorrows
That do attend a Soul in love like mine:
My Passion only fits the Object now;
I hate to tell you so, 'tis a poor low means
To gain a Mistress by, of so much wit:
Aminta, you're above that common rate
Of being won.
Mean Beauties should be flatter'd into praise,
Whilst you need only Sighs from every Lover,
To tell you who you conquer, and not how,
Nor to instruct you what attracts you have.

AMINTA - This will not serve to convince me,
But you have lov'd before.

ALCANDER - And will you never quit that error, Madam?

AMINTA - 'Tis what I've reason to believe, Alcander,
And you can give me none for loving me:
I'm much unlike Lucinda whom you sigh'd for,
I'm not so coy, nor so reserv'd as she;
Nor so designing as Florana your next Saint,
Who starv'd you up with hope, till you grew weary;
And then Ardelia did restore that loss,
The little soft Ardelia, kind and fair too.

ALCANDER - You think you're wondrous witty now, Aminta,
But hang me if you be.

AMINTA - Indeed, Alcander, no, 'tis simple truth:
Then for your bouncing Mistress, long Brunetta,
O that majestick Garb, 'tis strangely taking,
That scornful Look, and Eyes that strike all dead
That stand beneath them.

Alcander, I have none of all these Charms:
But well, you say you love me; could you be
Content to dismiss these petty sharers in your Heart,
And give it all to me; on these conditions
I may do much.

ALCANDER - Aminta, more perhaps than I may like.

AMINTA - Do not fear that, Alcander.

ALCANDER - Your Jealousy incourages that Fear.

AMINTA - If I be so, I'm the fitter for your humour.

ALCANDER - That's another reason for my fears; that ill-Luck owes us a spite, and will be sure to pay us with loving one another, a thought I dread. Farewel, Aminta; when I can get loose from Ardelia, I may chance wait on you, till then your own Pride be your Companion.

[Holds him.

AMINTA - Nay, you shall not go, Alcander.

ALCANDER - Fy on't, those Looks have lost their wonted Force,
I knew you'd call me back to smile upon me,
And then you have me sure; no, no, Aminta,
I'll no more of that.   [Goes out.

AMINTA - I have too much betray'd my Passion for him,
I must recal it, if I can I must:
I will, for should I yield, my power's o'erthrown,

And what's a Woman when that glory's gone?

[Exit.

SCENE II. The Apartments of Alcippus.

Enter Alcippus and Pisaro.

PISARO - You seem'd then to be pleas'd with what she said.

ALCIPPUS - And then methought I was so,
But yet even then I fear'd she did dissemble.
Gods, what's a Man possest with Jealousy?

PISARO - A strange wild thing, a Lover without reason;
I once have prov'd the torture on't,
But as unlike to thine as good from evil;
Like fire in Limbecks, mine was soft and gentle,
Infusing kindly heat, till it distill'd
The spirits of the Soul out at my Eyes,
And so it ended.
But thine's a raging Fire, which never ceases
Till it has quite destroy'd the goodly Edifice
Where it first took beginning.
Faith, strive, Sir, to suppress it.

ALCIPPUS - No, I'll let it run to its extent,
And see what then 'twill do.
Perhaps 'twill make me mad, or end my life,
Either of which will ease me.

PISARO - Neither of these, Alcippus;
It will unman you, make you too despis'd;
And those that now admire will pity you.

ALCIPPUS - What wouldst thou have me do?
Am I not ty'd a Slave to follow Love,
Whilst at my back Freedom and Honour waits,
And I have lost the power to welcome them?
Like those who meet a Devil in the night,
And all afrighted gaze upon the Fury,
But dare not turn their backs to what they fear,
Though safety lie behind them.
Alas! I would as willingly as those
Fly from this Devil, Love.

PISARO - You may, like those afrighted, by degrees
Allay your sense of terror in the Object,
And then its Power will lesson with your Fear,

And 'twill be easy to forgo the Fantasm.

ALCIPPUS - No, then like the damn'd Ghost it follows me.

PISARO - Let Reason then approach it, and examine it.

ALCIPPUS - Love is a surly and a lawless Devil,
And will not answer Reason.
I must encounter it some other way,
For I will lay the Fiend.

PISARO - What would you have, Alcippus?

ALCIPPUS - I'd have fair play, Pisaro.
I find the cheat, and will not to the Camp;
Thou shalt supply my place, and I'll return:
The Night grows on, and something will be done
That I must be acquainted with.

PISARO - Pardon me, Sir, if I refuse you here;
I find you're growing up to Jealousies,
Which I'll not trust alone with you.

ALCIPPUS - Thou know'st perhaps of something worthy it.

PISARO - I must confess, your Passions give me cause,
If I had any Secrets, to conceal them;
But 'tis no time nor place to make disputes in:
Will you to Horse?

ALCIPPUS - Will you not think fit I should return then?
I can be calm.

PISARO - What is't you mean by this return, Alcippus?

ALCIPPUS - To see Erminia, is not that enough
To one in love, as I am?

PISARO - But, Sir, suppose you find Philander there?

ALCIPPUS - Then I suppose I shall not much approve on't.

PISARO - You would be at your last night's rage again.
Alcippus, this will ruin you for ever,
Nor is it all the Power you think you have
Can save you, if he once be disoblig'd.
Believe me 'twas the Princess' passion for you
Made up that breach last night.

ALCIPPUS - All this I know as well as you, Pisaro,
But will not be abus'd; alas, I'm lost:

Could I recal these two last days are past,
Ah, I should be my self again, Pisaro.
I would refuse these Fetters which I wear,
And be a Slave to nothing but to Glory.

PISARO - That were a Resolution worthy of you.
But come, 'tis late, what you resolve conclude.

ALCIPPUS - I am resolv'd I will not to the Camp,
A secret inclination does persuade me
To visit my Erminia to night.

PISARO - Comes it from Love or Jealousy?

ALCIPPUS - The first, good faith, Pisaro; thou'rt so fearful
You shall to th'Camp before,
And I'll be with you early in the Morning.

PISARO - Give me your hand, and promise to be calm.

ALCIPPUS - By all our Friendships, as the Western Winds,
[Gives his hand.
Nothing that's done shall e'er inrage me more,
Honour's the Mistress I'll henceforth adore.
[Exit.

PISARO - I will not trust you though.

[Goes out another way.

SCENE III. The Court Gallery.

Enter Philander and Alcander in their Clokes
muffled as in the dark.

ALCANDER - Isillia.
[Calls at the lodgings of Erminia.

ISILLIA - [Entering.] Who's there?

ALCANDER - A Friend.

ISILLIA - My Lord Alcander?

ALCANDER - The same.

ISILLIA - Where's the Prince?

PHILANDER - Here, Isillia.

ISILLIA - Give me your hand, my Lord, and follow me.

PHILANDER - To such a Heaven as thou conduct'st me to,
Though thou should'st traverse Hell, I'd follow thee.

ALCANDER - You'll come back in charity, Isillia?

ISILLIA - Yes, if I dare trust you alone with me.

[They go all in.

SCENE IV.

Draws off, a Chamber, discovers Erminia in a dishabit, sitting; to her Philander, who falls at her feet, on his knees.

ERMINIA - My Lord the Prince, what makes your Highness here?

PHILANDER - Erminia, why do ask that needless question?
'Twas Love, Love that's unsatisfied, which brought me hither.
[Kneels.

ERMINIA - Rise, Sir, this posture would become me better.

PHILANDER - Permit me, dear Erminia, to remain thus.
'Tis only by these signs I can express
What my Confusion will not let me utter.
I know not what strange power thou bear'st about thee,
But at thy sight or touch my Sense forsakes me,
And that, withal I had design'd to say,
Turns to a strange disorder'd Rapture in me.
Oh Erminia

ERMINIA - How do you, Sir?

PHILANDER - I am not well;
Too suddenly I pass from one extreme
To this of Joy, more insupportable:
But I shall re-assume my health anon,
And tell thee all my story.

ERMINIA - Dear Sir, retire into this inner room,
And there repose awhile:
Alas, I see disorder in your Face.

PHILANDER - This confidence of me, is generous in thee.

[They go into the Scene which draws over.

SCENE V. The Court Gallery.

Enter Alcippus.

ALCIPPUS - The Night is calm and silent as my Thoughts,
Where nothing now but Love's soft whispers dwell;
Who in as gentle terms upbraids my Rage,
Which strove to dispossess the Monarch thence:
It tells me how dishonest all my Fears are,
And how ungrateful all my Jealousies;
And prettily persuades those Infidels
To be less rude and mutinous hereafter.
Ah, that I could remain in this same state,
And be contented with this Monarchy:
I would, if my wild multitude of Passions
Could be appeas'd with it; but they're for Liberty,
And nothing but a Common-wealth within
Will satisfy their appetites of Freedom.
Pride, Honour, Glory, and Ambition strive
How to expel this Tyrant from my Soul,
But all too weak, though Reason should assist them.
[He knocks. Alcander looks out at the door.

ALCANDER - Who's there?

ALCIPPUS - A Friend.

ISILLIA - [Within.] Oh Heavens! it is my Lord Alcippus' voice.

ALCANDER - Peace, Isillia.

ALCIPPUS - I hear a Man within, open the door.
Now, Love, defend thy Interest, or my Jealousy
Will grow the mightier Devil of the two else.   [Alcan. comes out.
Who's this? one muffled in a Cloke?
What art thou, who at this dead time of Night
Hast took possession here?
Speak, or I'll kill thee.

ALCANDER - This were an opportunity indeed
To do my Prince a service, but I dare not.

ALCIPPUS - What darest not do?

ALCANDER - Not kill thee.

ALCIPPUS - Is that thy business then? have at thee, Slave?
I'll spoil your keeping doors.   [Runs at him.

[They fight, and grapling, Alcander gets the Sword of Alcippus.

He'as got my Sword, however, I'll lose no time:
It may be 'tis his office to detain me.   [He goes in.

ALCANDER - I'm wounded, yet I will not leave him so;
There may be Mischief in him, though unarm'd.

[Goes in.

SCENE VI. A Bed-chamber.

Discovers Erminia, Philander sitting on the Bed, to them
Isillia, a Sword and Hat on the Table.

ISILLIA - Ah, Madam, Alcippus.

ERMINIA - Alcippus, where?

ISILLIA - I left him in a quarrel with Alcander,
And hear him coming up.

ERMINIA - For Heaven's sake, Sir, submit to be conceal'd.

PHILANDER - Not for the world, Erminia,
My Innocence shall be my guard and thine.

ERMINIA - Upon my knees I'll beg you'll be conceal'd,   [A noise.
He comes; Philander, for my safety go.

PHILANDER - I never did obey with more regret.

[He hides himself behind the Bed, and in haste leaves his Sword and Hat on the Table; Alcippus comes in.

ALCIPPUS - How now, Erminia?
How comes it you are up so late?

ERMINIA - I found my self not much inclin'd to sleep;
I hope 'tis no offence.
Why do you look so wildly round about you?

ALCIPPUS - Methinks, Erminia, you are much confus'd.

ERMINIA - Alas, you cannot blame me;
Isillia tells me you were much inrag'd
Against a Lover she was entertaining.

ALCIPPUS - A Lover, was that a time for Courtship?
Such Actions, Madam, will reflect on you.

[Isillia goes to take the Hat and Sword and slide
into her lap, which he sees, calls to her.

What have you there, Isillia?
Come back, and let me see what 'tis.
[He takes them from her.
Ha, a Sword and Hat, Erminia, whose be these?

ERMINIA - Why do you ask?

ALCIPPUS - To be inform'd, is that so great a wonder?

ERMINIA - They be my Father's, Sir.

ALCIPPUS - Was that well said, Erminia? speak again.

ERMINIA - What is't you would know?

ALCIPPUS - The truth, Erminia, 'twould become you best.
Do you think I take these things to be your Father's?
No, treacherous Woman, I have seen this Sword,
[Draws the Sword.
Worn by a Man more vigorous than thy Father,
It had not else been here.
Where have you hid this mighty Man of valour?
Have you exhausted so his stock of Courage,
He has not any left t'appear withal?

PHILANDER - Yes, base Alcippus, I have still that Courage,
Th'effects of which thou hast beheld with wonder;
And now being fortified by Innocence,
Thou't find sufficient to chastise thy boldness:
Restore my Sword, and prove the truth of this.

ALCIPPUS - I've hardly so much Calmness left to answer thee,
And tell thee, Prince, thou art deceiv'd in me.
I know 'tis just I should restore thy Sword,
But thou hast show'd the basest of thy play,
And I'll return th'uncivil Treachery;
You merit Death for this base Injury.
But you're my Prince, and that I own you so,
Is all remains in me of Sense or Justice;
The rest is Rage, which if thou gett'st not hence
Will eat up that small morsel too of Reason,
And leave me nothing to preserve thy life with.

PHILANDER - Gods, am I tame, and hear the Traytor brave me?
[Offers to run into him.

I have resentment left, though nothing else.

ALCIPPUS - Stand off, by all that's good, I'll kill thee else.
[Ermina puts her self between.

ERMINIA - Ah, hold, Sir, hold, the Prince has no defence,
And you are more than arm'd;   [To Alcip.
What honour is't to let him murder you?   [To the Prince.
Nor would your Fame be lessen'd by retreat.

PHILANDER - Alas, I dare not leave thee here with him.

ERMINIA - Trust me, Sir, I can make him calm again.

ALCIPPUS - She counsels well, and I advise you take it.

PHILANDER - I will, but not for fear of thee or Death,
But from th'assurance that her Power's sufficient
To allay this unbecoming Fury in thee,
And bring thee to repentance.

[He gives him his Sword; Philander goes out,
Alcippus locks the door after him.

ERMINA - Alcippus, what do you mean?

ALCIPPUS - To know where 'twas you learn'd this Impudence?
Which you're too cunning in,
Not to have been a stale practitioner.

ERMINIA - Alas, what will you do?

ALCIPPUS - Preserve thy Soul, if thou hast any sense
Of future Joys, after this vile damn'd Action.

ERMINIA - Ah, what have I done?

ALCIPPUS - That which if I should let thee live, Erminia,
Would never suffer thee to look abroad again.
Thou'st made thy self and me
Oh, I dare not name the Monsters.
But I'll destroy them while the Gods look down,
And smile upon my Justice.

[He strangles her with a Garter, which he snatches
from his Leg, or smothers her with a pillow.

ERMINIA - Hold, hold, and hear my Vows of Innocence.

ALCIPPUS - Let me be damn'd as thou art, if I do;
[Throws her on a Bed, he sits down in a Chair.

So now, my Heart, I have redeem'd thee nobly,
Sit down and pause a while
But why so still and tame, is one poor Murder
Enough to satisfy thy storm of Passion?
If it were just, it ought not here to end;
If not, I've done too much

[One knocks, he rises after a little pause,
and opens the door; enter Page.

PAGE - My Lord, Pisaro.

Alcip. Pisaro, Oh, that Name has wakened me,
A Name till now had never Terror in't!
I will not speak with him.

PAGE - My Lord, he's here.
[Page goes out.

Enter Pisaro.

PISARO - Not speak with me! nay then I fear the worst.

ALCIPPUS - Not for the world, Pisaro.

[Hides his face with his hand, Pis. sees Erminia.

PISARO - Thy guilt is here too plain,
I need not read it in thy blushing face,
She's dead and pale: Ah, sweet Erminia!

ALCIPPUS - If she be dead, the fitter she's for me,
She'll now be coy no more, nor cry I cannot love,
And frown and blush, when I but kiss her hand:
Now I shall read no terror in her Eyes,
And what is better yet, shall ne'er be jealous.

PISARO - Why didst thou make such haste to be undone?
Had I detain'd thee but an hour longer,
Thou'dst been the only happy of thy Sex.
I knew thou didst dissemble when we parted,
And therefore durst not trust thee with thy Passions:
I only staid to gather from my Sister
What news I might concerning your affairs,
Which I with joy came to impart to you,
But most unfortunately came too late:
Why didst thou yield obedience to that Devil,
Which urg'd thee to destroy this Innocent?

ALCIPPUS - Pisaro, do not err;
I found the Prince and she alone together,

He all disorder'd like a Ravisher,
Loose and unbutton'd for the amorous play;
O that she had another Life to lose!

PISARO - You wrong her most inhumanly, you do;
Her Blood, yet sensible of the injury,
Flows to her face to upbraid thy Cruelty.
Where dost thou mean, bad Man, to hide thy head?
Vengeance and Justice will pursue thee close,
And hardly leave thee time for Penitence.
What will the Princess say to this return
You've made to all the offers she has sent
This Night by Prince Philander?

ALCIPPUS - Oh, when you name the Princess and Philander,
Such different Passions do at once possess me,
As sink my over-laden Soul to Hell.
Alas, why do I live? 'tis losing time;
For what is Death, a pain that's sooner ended
Than what I felt from every frown of hers?
It was but now that lovely thing had Life,
Could speak and weep, and had a thousand Charms,
That had oblig'd a Murder, and Madness't self
To've been her tame Adorers.
Yet now should even her best belov'd, the Prince,
With all his Youth, his Beauties and Desires,
Fall at her Feet, and tell his tale of Love,
She hardly would return his amorous Smiles,
Or pay his meeting Kisses back again;
Is not that fine, Pisaro?

PISARO - Sir, 'tis no time to talk in, come with me,
For here's no safety for a Murderer.

ALCIPPUS - I will not go, alas I seek no Safety.

PISARO - I will not now dispute that vain reply,
But force you to security.

[Pisaro draws him out, the Scene closes.

SCENE VII. The Palace.

Enter Philander, Alcander, Galatea, Aminta, and Falatius.

FALATIUS - Ah, fly, Sir, fly from what I have to tell you.

ALCANDER - What's the news?

FALATIUS - Ah, Sir, the dismal'st heavy news that e'er was told or heard.

GALATEA - No matter, out with it.

FALATIUS - Erminia, Madam.

PHILANDER - Erminia, what of her?

FALATIUS - Is dead, Sir.

ALCANDER - What, hast thou lost thy Wits?

FALATIUS - I had them not about me at the sight,
I else had been undone: Alas, Erminia's dead,
Murder'd, and dead.

ALCANDER - It cannot be, thou ly'st.

FALATIUS - By Jove, I do not, Sir, I saw her dead:
Alas, I ran as I was wont to do,
Without demanding licence, to her Chamber,
But found her not, as I was wont to do,   [The Women weep.
In a gay humour, but stone-dead and cold.

PHILANDER - Alcander, am I awake? or being so,
Dost not perceive this senseless Flesh of mine
Hardened into a cold benumbed Statue?
Methinks it does-support me-or I fall;
And so-shall break to pieces
[Falls into his Arms. He leads him out.

GALATEA - Ah, lovely Maid, was this thy destiny?
Did Heaven create thy Beauties to this end?
I must distrust their Bounties, who neglected
The best and fairest of their handy-work;
This will incourage Sin, when Innocence
Must perish thus, and meet with no defence.

Enter the King and Orgulius.

ORGULIUS - If murder'd Innocence do cry for Justice,
Can you, great Sir, make a defence against it?

KING - I think I cannot.

ORGULIUS - Sir, as you are pious, as you are my King,
The Lover and Protector of your People,
Revenge Erminia's Murder on Alcippus.

GALATEA - If e'er my Mother, Sir, were dear to you,
As from your Tears I guest whene'er you nam'd her;

If the remembrance of those Charms remain,
Whose weak resemblance you have found in me,
For which you oft have said you lov'd me dearly;
Dispense your mercy, and preserve this Copy,
Which else must perish with th'Original.

KING - Why all this Conjuration, Galatea?

GALATEA - To move you, Sir, to spare Alcippus' Life.

KING - You are unjust, if you demand a Life
Must fall a Sacrifice to Erminia's Ghost,
That is a debt I have ingag'd to pay.

GALATEA - Sir, if that Promise be already past,
And that your Word be irrevocable,
I vow I will not live a moment after him.

KING - How, Galatea! I'd rather hop'd you'd join'd
Your Prayers with his.

GALATEA - Ah, Sir, the late Petition which I made you
Might have inform'd you why these Knees are bow'd;
'Twas but this night I did confess I lov'd him,
And you would have allow'd that Passion in me,
Had he not been Erminia's:
And can you question now what this Address meant?

ORGULIUS - Remember, Sir, Erminia was my Daughter.

GALATEA - And, Sir, remember that I am your Daughter.

ORGULIUS - And shall the Traitor live that murder'd her?

GALATEA - And will you by his Death, Sir, murder me?
In dear Erminia's Death too much is done;
If you revenge that Death, 'tis two for one.

ORGULIUS - Ah, Sir, to let him live's unjust in you.

GALATEA - And killing me, you more injustice do.

Org. Alcippus, Madam, merits not your Love,
That could so cruel to Erminia prove.

GALATEA - If Lovers could be rul'd by Reason's Laws,
For this complaint on him we'ad had no cause.
'Twas Love that made him this rash act commit;
Had she been kind, 't had taught him to submit.
But might it not your present Griefs augment,
I'd say that you deserve this punishment,

By forcing her to marry with the General;
By which you have destroy'd Philander too,
And now you would Alcippus' Life undo.

ORGULIUS - That was a fault of duty to your Majesty.

KING - Though that were honest, 'twere not wisely done;
For had I known the passion of my Son,
And how essential 'twas to his content
I willingly had granted my consent;
Her Worth and Beauty had sufficient been
T'ave rais'd her to the Title of a Queen.
Did not my glorious Father, great Gonzal,
Marry the Daughter of his Admiral?
And I might to my Son have been as kind,
As then my Father did my Grandsire find.

ORGULIUS - You once believ'd that I had guilty been,
And had the Punishment, but not the Sin;
I suffer'd when 'twas thought I did aspire,
And should by this have rais'd my crimes yet higher.

KING - How did Philander take Erminia's death?

GALATEA - My own surprize and grief was so extream,
I know not what effects it had in him;
But this account of him, I'm forc'd to give,
Since she is dead, I know he cannot live.

KING - I'll know Philander's fate e'er I proceed;
And if he die, Alcippus too shall bleed.

[Exeunt.

SCENE VIII. The Gallery.

Enter Falatius and Labree.

FALATIUS - Wert thou never valiant, Labree?

LABREE - Yes, Sir, before I serv'd you, and since too: I
Am provok'd to give you proofs on't sometimes;
For when I am angry I am a very Hector.

FALATIUS - Ay, the Devil when a body's angry, but that's
Not the Valour in mode; Men fight now a-days
Without that, and even embrace whilst they draw
Their Swords on one another.

LABREE - Ay, Sir, those are Men that despise their lives.

FALATIUS - Why, that's it, Labree, that I would learn to do,
And which I fear, nothing but Poverty will make me do;
Jove defend me from that experiment.

Enter Erminia veil'd with a thin Tiffany.

LABREE - What's the matter, Sir?
Does the fit take you now?

FALATIUS - Save us, save us, from the Fiend.

LABREE - A Ghost, a Ghost! O, O, O!

[They fall shaking on the ground.

ERMINIA - This was a happy mistake,
Now I may pass with safety.
[Ex.

FALATIUS - Look up, Labree, if thou hast any of that
Courage thou spakest of but now.

LABREE - I dare not, Sir, experience yours I pray.

FALATIUS - Alas, alas, I fear we are both rank Cowards.

LABREE - Rise, Sir, 'tis gone.

FALATIUS - This was worse than the fright Alcander put
Me into by much.

[They rise and go out.

SCENE IX. Philander's Apartments.

Enter Philander and Cleontius.

PHILANDER - I know he's fled to the Camp,
For there he only can secure himself.

CLEONTIUS - I do not think it, Sir.
He's too brave to justify an Action
Which was the Outrage only of his Passion,
That soon will toil it self into a Calm,
And then will grow considerate again,
And hate the Rashness it provok'd him to.

PHILANDER - That shall not serve his turn, go
Tell him I'll get his Pardon of the King,
And set him free from other fears of Justice,
But those which I intend to execute.
If he be brave, he'll not refuse this offer;
If not, I'll do as he has done by me,
And meet his hated Soul by Treachery. [Cleontius goes out.
And then I've nothing more to do but die.
Ah, how agreeable are the thoughts of Death!
How kindly do they entertain my Soul,
And tell it pretty tales of Satisfaction in the other world,
That I shall dwell for ever with Erminia? but stay,
That sacred Spirit yet is unreveng'd,
I'll send that Traitor's Soul to eternal Night,
Then mine shall take its so desired Flight. [Going out.

Enter Erminia, calls him.

ERMINIA - Return, Philander, whither wouldst thou fly?

PHILANDER - What Voice is that? [Turns, sees her, and is frighted.

ERMINIA - 'Tis I, my Prince, 'tis I.

PHILANDER - Thou-Gods-what art thou-in that lovely shape?

ERMINIA - A Soul that from Elysium made escape,
[As she comes towards him, he goes back in great amaze.
To visit thee; why dost thou steal away?
I'll not approach thee nearer than I may.

PHILANDER - Why do I shake, it is Erminia's form
And can that Beauty ought that's ill adorn?
In every part Erminia does appear,
And sure no Devil can inhabit there.

[He comes on and kneels, one knocks, she steals back in at a door.

ALCANDER - [Within.] My Lord the Prince!

PHILANDER - Ha. Oh Gods, I charge thee not to vanish yet!
I charge thee by those Powers thou dost obey,
Not to deprive me of thy blessed sight.

ERMINIA - I will revisit thee. [Ex.

Enter Alcander.

PHILANDER - I'm not content with that.
Stay, stay, my dear Erminia.

ALCANDER - What mean you, Sir?
[He rises and looks still afrighted.

PHILANDER - Alcander, look, look, how she glides away,
Dost thou not see't?

ALCANDER - Nothing, Sir, not I.

PHILANDER - No, now she's gone again.

ALCANDER - You are disorder'd, pray sit down a while.

PHILANDER - No, not at all, Alcander; I'm my self,
I was not in a Dream, nor in a Passion
When she appear'd, her Face a little pale,
But else my own Erminia, she her self,
I mean a thing as like, nay, it spoke too,
And I undaunted answer'd it again;
But when you knockt it vanisht.

ALCANDER - 'Twas this Aminta would persuade me to,
And, faith, I laught at her,
And wish I might have leave to do so now.

PHILANDER - You do displease me with your Unbelief.

ALCANDER - Why, Sir, do you think there can indeed be Ghosts?

PHILANDER - Pray do not urge my Sense to lose its nature.

ERMINIA - It is Alcander, I may trust him too.
[She peeps in on them, and comes out.

PHILANDER - Look where she comes again, credit thy Eyes,
Which did persuade thee that they saw her dead.

ALCANDER - By Heaven, and so they did.
[Both seem frighted.
Gods, this is wondrous strange! yet I can bear it,
If it were the Devil himself in that fair shape.

PHILANDER - And yet thou shakest.

ALCANDER - I do, but know not why.
Inform us, lovely Spirit, what thou art,
A God or Devil; if either, thou art welcome.

ERMINIA - You cannot think, Alcander, there be Ghosts.
[She gives her hands to him and Phi. which
they refuse to touch.
No, give me your hand, and prove mine flesh and blood.

Sir, you were wont to credit what I said,
And I would still merit that kind opinion.

PHILANDER - Erminia, Soul of Sweetness, is it you?
How do you ravish with excess of Joys?

ERMINIA - Softly, dear Sir, do not express that Joy,
Lest you destroy it by your doing so.
I fly for sanctuary to your Arms;
As yet none knows I live, but poor Isillia,
Who bathing of my cold face with her tears,
Perceiv'd some signs of life, and us'd what means
Her Love and Duty did instruct her in;
And I in half an hour was so reviv'd,
As I had sense of all was past and done;
And to prevent a death I yet might fear,
If mad Alcippus had return'd again,
Alone I came to you, where I could find
Alone my Safety too.

PHILANDER - From Gods and Men, Erminia, thou art safe,
My best and blest Erminia.

ERMINIA - Sir, in my coming hither I met Aminta,
Who I may fear has alarm'd all the Court;
She took me for a Ghost, and ran away,
E'er I cou'd undeceive her.
Falatius too, afrighted even to death

ALCANDER - Faith, that was lucky, Madam.
Hark, some body knocks, you'd best retire a little.
[Leads her into the door.

Enter Galatea and Aminta lighted.

GALATEA - Ah, Brother, there's such news abroad.

PHILANDER - What, dear Sister, for I am here confin'd,
And cannot go to meet it?

GALATEA - Erminia's Ghost is seen, and I'm so frighted.

PHILANDER - You would not fear it though it should appear.

GALATEA - Oh, do not say so;
For though the World had nought I held more dear,
I would not see her Ghost for all the World.

ALCANDER - But, Madam, 'tis so like Erminia -

AMINTA - Why, have you seen it too?

ALCANDER - Yes, Aminta.

AMINTA - Then there be Ghosts, Alcander.

PHILANDER - Aminta, we'll convince him.
[Phi. leads out Er. who comes smiling to the Princess.

GALATEA - But how, dear Creature, wert thou thus preserv'd?

PHILANDER - Another time for that, but now let's think
[Aminta embraces her.
How to preserve her still.
Since all believe her dead, but who are present,
And that they may remain in that blest error,
I will consult with you; but you, my dearest,
Shall as the Spirit of Erminia act,
And reap the glory of so good a part:
It will advance the new design I have;
And, Sister, to your care
I must commit the Treasure of my Life.

GALATEA - It was not kind, she came not first to me.

ERMINIA - Madam, I fear'd the safety of my Prince,
And every moment that I found I liv'd,
Were more tormenting than those of death,
Till I had undeceiv'd his Apprehensions.

PHILANDER - 'Twas like thy self, generous and kind, my Dear,
Thou mightst have come too late else.

ERMINIA - But, Sir, pray where's my Murderer? for yet
A better name I cannot well afford him.

GALATEA - All that we know of him,
Pisaro now inform'd me,
Who came just as he thought he had murder'd thee,
And begg'd he would provide for his own safety.
But he who gave him sober promises,
No sooner found himself out of his arms,
But frantick and i'th' dark he got away.
But out o'th' Court he knows he cannot pass
At this dead time of night;
But he believes he is i'th' Groves or Gardens,
And thither he is gone to find him out.

ALCANDER - This is no place to make a longer stay in,
The King has many Spies about the Prince,
'Twere good you would retire to your Apartment.

GALATEA - We'll take your Counsel, Sir.
Good night, Brother.

PHILANDER - Erminia, may thy Dreams be calm and sweet,
As thou hast made my Soul;
May nothing of the Cruelty that's past,
Approach thee in a rude uneasy thought;
Remember it not so much as in thy Prayers,
Let me alone to thank the Gods for thee,
To whom that Blessing only was ordain'd.

And when I lose my Gratitude to Heaven,
May they deprive me of the Joys they've given.

[Exeunt.

ACT V.

SCENE I. Galatea's Apartments.

Enter Galatea, Erminia, Pisaro, Aminta.

GALATEA - And hast thou found him? Ease my misery.

PISARO - I have, and done as you commanded me.
I found him sitting by a Fountain side,
Whose Tears had power to swell the little tide,
Which from the Marble Statues breasts still flows:
As silent and as numberless were those.
I laid me down behind a Thicket near,
Where undiscover'd I could see and hear;
The Moon the Day supply'd, and all below
Instructed, even as much as Day could do.
I saw his postures, heard him rave and cry,
'Twas I that kill'd Erminia, yes 'twas I;
Then from his almost frantick Head he'd tear
Whole handfuls of his well-becoming Hair:
Thus would he, till his Rage was almost spent,
And then in softer terms he would lament:
Then speak as if Erminia still did live,
And that Belief made him forget to grieve.
The Marble Statue Venus he mistook
For fair Erminia, and such things he spoke,
Such unheard passionate things, as e'en wou'd move
The marble Statue's self to fall in love;
He'd kiss its Breast, and say she kind was grown,
And never mind, alas, 'twas senseless Stone;
He took its Hand, and to his Mouth had laid it,
But that it came not, and its stay betray'd it;

Then would he blush, and all asham'd become,
His Head declining, for awhile be dumb:
His Arms upon his Breast across would lay,
Then sensibly and calmly walk away;
And in his walk a thousand things he said,
Which I forgot, yet something with me staid;
He did consult the nature of the Crime,
And still concluded that 'twas just in him;
He run o'er all his life, and found no act
That was ungenerous in him, but this fact,
From which the Justice took off the Disgrace,
And might even for an act of Virtue pass;
He did consult his Glory and his Pride;
And whilst he did so, laid his grief aside;
Then was as calm as e'er he seem'd to be.

GALATEA - And all this while did he ne'er mention me?

PISARO - Yes, Madam, and a thousand things he said,
By which much Shame and Passion he betray'd:
And then 'twas, Madam, I stept in and gave
Counsels, I thought him fittest to receive;
I sooth'd him up, and told him that the Crime
I had committed, had the case been mine.
I all things said that might his Griefs beguile,
And brought him to the sweetness of a Smile.
To all I said he lent a willing ear,
And my reproaches too at last did hear.
With this insensibly I drew him on,
And with my flatteries so upon him won,
Such Gentleness infus'd into his Breast,
As has dispos'd his wearied Soul to rest:
Sleeping upon a Couch I've left him now,
And come to render this account to you.   [Bows.

GALATEA - Pisaro, 'twas the office of a Friend,
And thou'st perform'd it to a generous end:
Go on and prosper in this new design,
And when thou'st done, the glory shall be thine.

[Exeunt.

SCENE II. The Bedchamber of Alcippus.

Draws off, discovers Alcippus rising from the Couch.

ALCIPPUS - I cannot sleep, my Soul is so unfurnish'd
Of all that Sweetness which allow'd it rest.
'Tis flown, 'tis flown, for ever from my breast,

And in its room eternal discords dwell,
Such as outdo the black intrigues of Hell
Oh my fortune.

[Weeps, pulling out his handkerchief, drops a Picture with a Glass on the reverse.

What's here? Alas, that which I dare not look on,
And yet, why should I shun that Image here,
Which I continually about me bear?
But why, dear Picture, art thou still so gay,
Since she is gone from whom those Charms were borrow'd?
Those Eyes that gave this speaking life to thine,
Those lovely Eyes are clos'd in endless darkness;
There's not a Star in all the face of Heaven,
But now out-shines those Suns:
Suns at Noon-day dispens'd not kindlier influence.
And thou blest Mirror, that hast oft beheld
That Face, which Nature never made a fairer;
Thou that so oft her Beauties back reflected,
And made her know what wondrous power there lay
In every Feature of that lovely Face.
But she will smile no more! no more! no more!
Why, who shall hinder her? Death, cruel Death.
'Twas I that murder'd her -
Thou lyest, thou durst as well be damn'd as touch her,
She was all sacred; and that impious Hand
That had profanely touch'd her,
Had wither'd from the Body.
I lov'd her, I ador'd her, and could I,
Could I approach her with unhallowed thoughts?
No, no, I durst not -
But as devoutest Pilgrims do the Shrine.
If I had done't,
The Gods who take the part of Innocence,
Had been reveng'd .
Why did not Thunder strike me in the Action?
Why, if the Gods be just, and I had done't,
Did they not suffer Earth to swallow me,
Quick, quick into her bosom?
But yet I say again, it was not I,
Let me behold this face,
That durst appear in such a Villany.
[He looks in the glass.

Enter Pisaro, and Erminia drest like an Angel with Wings.

PISARO - Look where he is.

ERMINIA - Alas, I tremble at the sight of him.

PISARO - Fear nothing, Madam, I'll be near you still.

ERMINIA - Pray stay a little longer.

ALCIPPUS - My Face has Horror in't pale and disfigur'd,
And lean as Envy's self
My Eyes all bloody, and my hanging lids
Like Midnight's mischief, hide the guilty Balls,
And all about me calls me Murderer:
Oh horrid Murderer!
That very Sound tears out my hated Soul,
And to compleat my ruin,
I'll still behold this face where Murder dwells.

[He looks in the glass, Erminia steals behind him, and looks into it over his shoulder; he is frighted.

Ha, what does this Glass present me?
What art thou? Speak. What art thou?
[Turns by degrees towards it.
Sure I am fixt, what, shall the Devil fright me?
Me shall he fright,
Who stood the Execution of a Murder?
But 'tis that Shape, and not thy Nature frights me,
That calls the blood out of my panting Heart,
That Traytor Heart that did conspire thy death.

ERMINIA - Sit down and hear me.

[In a tone like a Spirit, and points to a Chair; soft Musick begins to play, which continues all this Scene.

To disobey, thy punishment shall be;
To live in endless torments, but ne'er die.

ALCIPPUS - Thou threatnest high, bold Rebel,
[He sits within the Scene, bows.

ERMINIA - Alcippus, tell me what you see,
What is't that I appear to be?

ALCIPPUS - My blest Erminia deify'd.

ERMINIA - Alcippus, you inform me true;
I am thus deify'd by you;
To you I owe this blest abode,
For I am happy as a God;
I only come to tell thee so,
And by that tale to end thy Woe;
Know, Mighty Sir, your Joy's begun,
From what last night to me was done;
In vain you rave, in vain you weep,

For what the Gods must ever keep;
In vain you mourn, in vain deplore
A loss which tears can ne'er restore.
The Gods their Mercies will dispense,
In a more glorious Recompence;
A World of Blessings they've in store,
A World of Honours, Vict'ries more;
Thou shalt the Kingdom's Darling be,
And Kings shall Homage pay to thee;
Thy Sword no bounds to Conquest set,
And thy Success that Sword shall whet;
Princes thy Chariot-wheel shall grace,
Whilst thou in Triumph bring'st home Peace.

This will the Gods; thy King yet more
Will give thee what those Gods adore;
And what they did create for thee,
Alcippus, look, for that is she.

Enter the Princess, who goes over the Stage as a Spirit, bows a little to Alcippus, and goes off.

ALCIPPUS - The Princess!   [He offers to rise.

ERMINIA - Be still; 'tis she you must possess,
'Tis she must make your happiness;
'Tis she must lead you on to find
Those Blessings Heaven has design'd:
'Tis she'll conduct you, where you'll prove
The perfect Joys of grateful Love.

Enter Aminta like Glory, Alcander representing Honour.
They pass over and bow, and go out.

Glory and Honour wait on her.

Enter two more representing Mars and Pallas, bow and go out.

With Pallas and the God of War,

Enter Olinda like Fortune, a Page like Cupid, bow and go out.

Fortune and Love which ne'er agree,
Do now united bow to thee.
Be wise, and of their Bounties share;
For if Erminia still was here,
Still subject to the toils of Life,
She never could have been thy Wife,
Who by the Laws of Men and Heaven
Was to another's bosom given:
And what Injustice thou hast done,
Was only to thy Prince alone;

But he has mercy, can redeem
Those Ills which thou hast done to him.
But see, they all return again.

[All the Disguis'd enter again and dance, with Love in the midst, to whom as they dance, they in order make an offer of what they carry, which must be something to represent them by; which Love refuses with Nods, still pointing to Alcippus: the Dance done, they lay them at his feet, or seem to do so, and go out.

What think'st thou of thy Destiny,
Is't not agreeable to thee?
Tell me, Alcippus, is't not brave?
Is it not better than a Grave?
Cast off your Tears, abandon Grief,
And give what you have seen belief.
Dress all your Looks, and be as gay
As Virgins in the Month of May;
Deck up that Face where Sorrow grows,
And let your Smiles adorn your brows;
Recal your wonted Sweetness home,
And let your Eyes all Love become:
For what the Gods have willed and said,
Thou hast no power to evade.
What they decree none can withstand,
You must obey what they command.

[She goes out, he remains immoveable for a while.

Enter Pisaro.

PISARO - How is it, man? what, speechless?

ALCIPPUS - No.

PISARO - I left thee on the Bed, how camest thou here?

ALCIPPUS - I know not.

PISARO - Have you slept?

ALCIPPUS - Yes, ever since you left me;
And 'twas a kindness in thee now to wake me;
For Sleep had almost flatter'd me to Peace,
Which is a vile injustice.
Hah, Pisaro, I had such a Dream,
Such a fine flattering Dream

PISARO - How was it, pray?

ALCIPPUS - Nay, I will forget it;
I do not merit so much peace of mind,

As the relation of that Dream will give me:
Oh, 'twas so perfect, too,
I hardly can persuade my self I slept!
Dost thou believe there may be Apparitions?

PISARO - Doubtless, my Lord, there be.

ALCIPPUS - I never could believe it till this hour,
By Heavens, I think I saw them too, Pisaro.

PISARO - 'Tis very possible you're not deceiv'd.

ALCIPPUS - Erminia's Spirit, in a glorious form.

PISARO - I do believe you.

ALCIPPUS - Why, is't not strange?

PISARO - It would have been, had I not heard already
She has this night appear'd to several Persons,
In several Shapes; the first was to the Prince;
And said so many pretty things for you,
As has persuaded him to pardon you.

ALCIPPUS - Oh Gods, what Fortune's mine!
I do believe the Prince is innocent
From all that thou hast said.
But yet I wish he would dispose his Bounties
On those that would return acknowledgments;
I hate he should oblige me.

PISARO - You are too obstinate, and must submit.

ALCIPPUS - It cannot be, and yet methinks I give
A strange and sudden credit to this Spirit,
It beckon'd me into another room;
I'll follow it, and know its business there.   [Aside.

PISARO - Come, Sir, I am a kind of Prophet,
And can interpret Dreams too.
We'll walk a while, and you shall tell me all,
And then I would advise you what to do.

[Exeunt.

SCENE III. The King's Chamber.

Enter Philander with the King.

KING - Thou'st entertain'd me with a pretty Story,
And call'd up so much Nature to thy Cause,
That I am half subjected to its Laws;
I find thy lovely Mother plead within too,
And bids me put no force upon thy Will;
Tells me thy Flame should be as unconfin'd
As that we felt when our two Souls combin'd.
Alas, Philander, I am old and feeble,
And cannot long survive:
But thou hast many Ages yet to number
Of Youth and Vigour; and should all be wasted
In the Embraces of an unlov'd Maid?
No, my Philander, if that after death
Ought could remain to me of this World's Joys,
I should remember none with more delight,
Than those of having left thee truly happy.

PHILANDER - This Goodness, Sir, resembles that of Heaven,
Preserving what it made, and can be paid
Only with grateful Praise as we do that.

KING - Go, carry on your innocent design,
And when you've done, the last act shall be mine.

[Exeunt

SCENE IV. The Court Gallery.

Enter Aminta followed by Alcander, Erminia and Galatea; they go out: re-enter Alcander, and stays Aminta.

ALCANDER - Stay, dear Aminta, do not fly so fast.

AMINTA - Methinks, Alcander, you should shun that Maid,
Of whose too much of kindness you're afraid.
'Twas not long since you parted in such feud,
And swore my treatment of you was too rude;
You vow'd you found no Beauty in my eyes,
And can you now pursue what you despise?   [Offers to go.

ALCANDER - Nay, do not leave me yet, for still your Scorn
Much better than your Absence may be borne.

AMINTA - Well, Sir, your business, for mine requires haste.

ALCANDER - Say, fair Aminta, shall I never find
You'll cease this Rigour, and be kind?
Will that dear Breast no Tenderness admit?
And shall the Pain you give no Pity get?

Will you be never touch'd with what I say?
And shall my Youth and Vows be thrown away?
You know my Passion and my Humour too,
And how I die, though do not tell you so.

AMINTA - What arguments will you produce to prove
You love? for yet I'll not believe you love.

ALCANDER - Since, fair Aminta, I did thee adore,
Alas, I am not what I was before:
My Thoughts disorder'd from my Heart do break;
And Sighs destroy my Language when I speak.
My Liberty and my Repose I gave,
To be admitted but your Slave;
And can you question such a Victory?
Or must I suffer more to make it sure?
It needs not, since these Languishments can be
Nought but the Wounds which you alone can cure.

AMINTA - Alcander, you so many Vows have paid,
So many Sighs and Tears to many a Maid,
That should I credit give to what you say,
I merit being undone as well as they.
No, no, Alcander, I'll no more of that.

ALCANDER - Farewel, Aminta, mayst thou want a Lover,
When I shall hate both thee and thy whole Sex;
I can endure your sober Cruelty,
But do despise it clad in Jollity.

[Exeunt severally.

SCENE V.

Discovers a Room hung with Black, a Hearse standing in it with Tapers round about it, Alcippus weeping at it, with Isillia, and other Women with long black Veils round about the Hearse.

ISILLIA - I humbly beg, my Lord, you would forbear.

ALCIPPUS - Oh Isillia,
Thou knowest not what vast Treasure this incloses,
This sacred Pile; is there no Sorrow due to it?
Alas, I bad her not farewel at parting.
Nor did receive so much as one poor Kiss.
Ah wretched, wretched Man!

Enter the Prince.

How, the Prince!

How suddenly my Grief submits to Rage.

PHILANDER - Alcippus, why dost thou gaze thus on me?
What Horror have I in my looks that frights thee?

ALCIPPUS - Why, Sir, what makes you here?
I have no more Wives, no more Erminias;
Alas, she is dead -
Will you not give her leave to rest in peace?

PHILANDER - Is this the Gratitude you pay my Favours,
That gave ye life, after your wrongs to me?
But 'twas my Sister's Kindness that preserv'd thee
And I prefer'd my Vengeance to the Gods.

ALCIPPUS - Your Sister is a Saint whom I adore;
But I refuse a Life that comes from you.

ISILLIA - What mean you, Sir?

ALCIPPUS - To speak a truth, as dying Men should do.

PHILANDER - Alcippus, for my Sister's sake who loves you,
I can bear more than this, you know my power,
And I can make you fear.   [Offers to go out.

ALCIPPUS - No, Prince, not whilst I am in love with dying.

PHILANDER - Your love to that I see has made you impudent.

ISILLIA - The Storm comes on, your Highness should avoid it.

PHILANDER - Let him give place, I'll keep possession here.

ISILLIA - It is the Prince's pleasure, Sir, you quit the Presence.

ALCIPPUS - No, this I call my Home;
And since Erminia's here that does entitle it so,
I will not quit the Presence.

PHILANDER - Gave thee a Title to't, Alcippus?

ALCIPPUS - Me, Philander!

[They come to each other's breast, and so draw.

PHILANDER - Thee.

ALCIPPUS - Me, what dare you now?

PHILANDER - I dare declare that I can hear no more;

Be witness, Heaven, how justly I'm compell'd.

ALCIPPUS - Now, Sir, you are brave and love Erminia too.

[The Women run all away crying; they draw out some one way, and some another, leaving some their Veils behind them, some half off, half on.

PHILANDER - We are here not safe, these Women will betray us.

ALCIPPUS - Sir, 'tis a work that will soon be dispatcht,
And this a place and time most proper for't.

[A pass or two. Fal. peeps in and runs away.

Enter Pisaro, runs between.

PISARO - Hold, Sir, are you grown desperate?
What means your Highness?   [To the Prince.
Alcippus, what is't you design in this?

ALCIPPUS - To fight, Pisaro, and be kill'd.

PISARO - By Heaven, you shall not fight, unless with me,
And you have so anger'd me with this rash action,
I could almost provoke you to it.

Enter Alcander.

ALCANDER - Gods, Sir, that you should thus expose your self,
The World's great Heir, against a desperate Madman!

PISARO - Have you forgot your Apparition, Sir?

ALCIPPUS - Oh, 'twas an idle lying one, Pisaro,
And came but to intrap me.

To them Galatea, Aminta, and Olinda.

GALATEA - Ah, Brother, why so cruel to your Sister?

PHILANDER - Here, Galatea, punish my misfortune,
For yet I want the will to injure thee.
Heaven knows what provocations I receiv'd
E'er I would draw a Sword on him you lov'd.

GALATEA - Unjust Alcippus, how dost thou reward me?

ALCIPPUS - Ah, Madam, I have too much shame to live.
Had Heaven preserv'd my Innocence intire,
That I with confidence might have ador'd you,
Though I had been successless;

Yet I had liv'd and hop'd, and aim'd to merit you:
But since all hopes of that are taken from me,
My Life is but too poor a Sacrifice,
To make atonement for my Sins to you.

GALATEA - I will not answer thee to what thou hast said,
But only beg thou wilt preserve thy life,
Without which mine will be of little use to me.

ALCIPPUS - Might I without a sin believe this Blessing,
Sure I should be immortal.

Falatio peeps in again.

FALATIUS - I think I may venture, the fury is past,
And the great shot spent, the mad
Captain General's wounded; so, I hope 'twill let out
Some of his hot blood

Enter the King, Cleontius, and Attendants.

KING - My Love, Alcippus, is despis'd I see,
And you in lieu of that return you owe me,
Endeavour to destroy me.
Is this an Object for your Rage to work on?
Behold him well, Alcippus, 'tis your Prince.
Who dares gaze on him with irreverend Eyes?
The good he does you ought to adore him for,
But all his evils 'tis the Gods must punish,
Who made no Laws for Princes.

ALCIPPUS - Sir, I confess I'm culpable,
And were it not a sin equal to that,
To doubt you could forgive me,
I durst not hope your mercy after it.

KING - I think with all the Tenderness I'm guilty of,
I hardly shall be brought to pardon thee.

PHILANDER - I humbly beg you will forgive him, Sir,
I drew him to it against his will; I forc'd him,
And gave him language not to be indur'd
By any gallant man.

KING - Whilst you intreat for him, who pleads for you?
For you are much the guiltier of the two,
And need'st a greater interest to persuade me.

ALCIPPUS - It were not just to contradict my Prince,
A Prince to whom I've been so late a Traitor;
But, Sir, 'tis I alone am criminal,

And 'twas I,
Justly I thought provok'd him to this hazard:
'Tis I was rude, impatient, insolent,
Did like a Madman animate his Anger,
Not like a generous Enemy.
Sir, when you weigh my Sorrows with this Action,
You'll find no base Design, no Villany there;
But being weary of a Life I hated,
I strove to put it off, and missing that way,
I come to make an offer of it here.

KING - If I should take it, 'twere no more than just;
Yet once again I will allow it thee,
That thou mayst owe me for't a second time:
Manage it better than the last I gave
[Ex. King.

PHILANDER - Alcippus, may I credit what thou'st said,
Or do you feign repentance to deceive me?

ALCIPPUS - I never could dissemble at my best,
And now methinks your Highness should believe me,
When my despairs and little love to life
Make me despise all ways that may preserve it.

PHILANDER - If thou wouldst have me credit thee, Alcippus,
Thou shouldst not disesteem a Life, which ought
To be preserv'd, to give a proof that what thou say'st
Is true, and dispossess me of those fears I have,
That 'tis my Life makes thine displeasing to thee.

ALCIPPUS - 'Tis a high proof to give you of my Duty,
Yet that's more ease to me than your Unbelief.

PHILANDER - Let me embrace and thank thee for this goodness.
[He offers to embrace him, but he is shy, and keeps a little off.
Why dost receive me coldly? I'm in earnest;
As I love Honour, and esteem thee generous,
I mean thee nothing but a perfect Friendship;
By all my hopes I've no more quarrels to thee,
All ends in this Embrace, and to confirm it
I give thee here my Sister to thy Wife.

ALCIPPUS - Your Pardon, Sir,
I must refuse your bounty, till I know
By what strange turn of Fate I came thus blest.
To you, my Prince, I've done unheard-of injuries,
And though your Mercy do afford me life,
With this rich present too;
Till I could know I might deserve them both,
That Life will prove a Plague, and this great Gift

Turn to the torment of it.

PHILANDER - Alcippus, 'tis not kind to doubt me still,
Is this a present for a Man I hate?

ALCIPPUS - 'Tis true, Sir, and your bounty does amaze me;
Can I receive a blessing of this magnitude
With hands, yet have not wash'd away the sin
Of your Erminia's murder? think of that, Sir;
For though to me it did appear most just,
Yet you must hate the Man that has undone you.

GALATEA - I see Erminia still usurps your thoughts.

ALCIPPUS - I must confess my Soul is scarce diverted
Of that fond Passion which I had for her;
But I protest before the Gods and you,
Did she still live, and I might still possess her,
I would refuse it, though I were ignorant
Of what the Gods and your fair self design me.

PHILANDER - To doubt thee were a sin below my nature,
And to declare my faith above my fear,
Behold what I present thee with.

[Goes out, and enters again with Erminia.

ALCIPPUS - Ha, Erminia?   [He looks afrighted.
It is the same appear'd to me last night,
And my deluded Fancy
Would have persuaded me 'twas but a dream.

PHILANDER - Approach her, Sir, 'tis no fantasm.

ALCIPPUS - 'Tis she her self, Oh Gods, Erminia!
[She goes a little back, as afraid, he kneels.
Ah, Madam, do not fear me in this posture,
Which I will never quit till you have pardon'd me;
It was a fault the most excusable,
That ever wretched Lover did commit;
And that which hinder'd me from following thee,
Was that I could not well repent the Crime;
But like a surly Sinner fac'd it out,
And said, I thought 'twas just, yes, fair Erminia;
Hadst thou been mine, I would i'th' face of Heaven,
Proclaim it just and brave revenge:
But, Madam, you were Wife to my Prince,
And that was all my sin:
Alas, in vain I hop'd for some return,
And grew impatient of th'unkind delay,
And franticky I then out-run my happiness.

ERMINIA - Rise, I forgive thee, from my soul I do;
Mayst thou be happier
In thy more glorious Passion for the Princess,
And all the Joys thou e'er couldst hope from me,
Mayst thou find there repeated.

Enter King, Orgulius, and the rest.

ORGULIUS - First, I'll keep my word with thee,
Receive the welcome present which I promis'd.

[Gives him Erminia, she kneels.

ERMINIA - Can you forgive the Griefs I've made you suffer?

ORGULIUS - I can forgive, though 'twas not kind
To let me languish in a desperate Error;
Why was this Blessing hid from me alone?

ERMINIA - Ah, Sir, so well I knew you lov'd Alcippus,
That had you known it e'er the Prince had own'd me,
I fear you had restor'd me back again,
A Sin too great to load your Soul withal.

ORGULIUS - My King already has forgiven that Error,
And now I come to make my Peace with thee,
And that I may with greatest speed obtain it,
To you, Sir, I resign her with as much Joy,   [To the Prince.
And when they undeceiv'd me
Of my opinion of her being dead -

PHILANDER - And I with greater Joy receive your gift.
[Bows and takes her.

KING - My Lord Alcippus, are you pleas'd with this?

ALCIPPUS - Sir, I am so pleas'd, so truly pleas'd with it,
That Heaven, without this Blessing on my Prince,
Had found but little trouble from my thanks,
For all they have shower'd on me;
'Twas all I wisht, next my Pretensions here.

KING - Then to compleat thy happiness,
Take Galatea, since her Passion merits thee,
As do thy Virtues her.

[Gives him Galatea they both bow.

ERMINIA - Sir, I've an humble suit t'your Majesty.

KING - Conclude it granted then.

ERMINIA - Falatius, Sir, has long made love t' Isillia,
And now he'as gain'd her Heart, he slights the Conquest,
Yet all the fault he finds is that she's poor.

KING - Isillia's Beauty can supply that want;
Falatius, what d'ye say to't?

FALATIUS - By Jove, Sir, I'll agree to any thing; for I believe a
handsome young Wife at Court may bring a Man a greater Fortune
than he can in Conscience desire.
[Takes Isillia.

ERMINIA - Aminta, be persuaded.   [Aside to Am.

AMINTA - He'd use me scurvily then.

ALCANDER - That's according as you behav'd yourself, Aminta.

AMINTA - I should domineer.

ALCANDER - I then should make love elsewhere.

AMINTA - Well, I find we shall not agree then.

ALCANDER - Faith, now we have disputed a point I never thought on
before, I would willingly pursue it for the humour on't, not that
I think I shall much approve on't.

PISARO - Give him your hand, Aminta, and conclude,
'Tis time this haughty humour were subdu'd.
By your submission, whatsoe'er he seem,
In time you'll make the greater Slave of him.

AMINTA - Well, not from the hope of that, but from my Love,
His change of humour I'm content to prove.
Here take me, Alcander;
Whilst to Inconstancy I bid adieu,
I find variety enough in you.

[He takes her and bows.

KING - Come my brave Youths, we'll toil our selves with Joys,
And when we're weary of the lazy play,
We'll search abroad to find new Conquests out,
And get fresh Appetites to new Delights:
It will redouble your vast stock of Courage,
And make th' uneasy Humour light and gentle;
When you remember even in heat of Battle,
That after all your Victories and Spoil,

You'll meet calm Peace at home in soft Embraces.
Thus may you number out your happy years,

Till Love and Glory no more proofs can give
Of what they can bestow, or you receive.

[Exeunt.

EPILOGUE,
By a Woman.

We charged you boldly in our first advance,
And gave the Onset à la mode de France,
As each had been a Joan of Orleance.

Like them our Heat as soon abated too;
Alas we could not vanquish with a Show,
Much more than that goes to the conquering you.

The Trial though will recompense the Pain,
It having wisely taught us how to reign;
'Tis Beauty only can our Power maintain.

But yet, as tributary Kings, we own
It is by you that we possess that Throne,
Where had we Victors been, we'ad reign'd alone.

And we have promised what we could not do;
A fault, methinks, might be forgiven too,
Since 'tis but what we learnt of some of you.

But we are upon equal treatment yet,
For neither conquer, since we both submit;
You to our Beauty bow, we to your Wit.

Aphra Behn – A Short Biography

Aphra Behn was baptised on December 14th in 1640.

Although she was a prolific and well established writer in her own lifetime facts about her remain scant and difficult to confirm. What can safely be said though is that Aphra Behn is now regarded as a key English playwright and a major figure in Restoration theatre

In fact even where and to whom she was born are subject to discussion.

According to which account you read – and there are many – Aphra was born in Harbledown, near Canterbury. Another that she was born to a barber, John Amis and his wife Amy. Or again she was born to a couple named Cooper.

In the "The Histories And Novels of the Late Ingenious Mrs. Behn" (1696) it is written that Aphra was born to Bartholomew Johnson, a barber, and Elizabeth Denham, a wet-nurse. However a claim by Colonel Thomas Colepeper, who states he knew her as a child, wrote in Adversaria that she was born at "Sturry or Canterbury" to a Mr Johnson and that she had a sister named Frances. Anne Kingsmill Finch, Countess of Winchilsea, a poetic contemporary, says that Aphra was born in Wye in Kent, and was the 'Daughter to a Barber.'

None of these accounts can be relied upon and it follows that with so few facts the early part of her life cannot be clearly illustrated.

However what can be accurately suggested is that Aphra was born in the rising tensions to the English Civil War. Obviously a time of much division and difficulty as the King and Parliament, and their respective forces, came ever closer to conflict.

But still facts do not reveal themselves in any quantity. As a young woman a version exists of Aphra's journeying to Surinam with Bartholomew Johnson. He was said to have died on the journey, leaving his wife and children spending some months in the country. It is during this trip that Aphra claims to have met an African slave leader. These experiences formed the basis for one of her most famous works, "Oroonoko". In "Oroonoko" Behn Aphra gifts herself the position of narrator and her first biographer accepted the proposition that Aphra was indeed the daughter of the lieutenant general of Surinam, as in the story. There is little evidence to support this case, and none of her contemporaries acknowledge this, or any, aristocratic status. There is also no evidence that Oroonoko existed as an actual person or that any such slave revolt, is anything but an invention.

However it is possible that she acted a spy in the colony. Possibilities exist. Perhaps Aphra re-wrote her own history as and when it suited her needs at the time.

The common method of gathering information in these times was Church records and for a few, tax records. Aphra Behn is mentioned in neither. As well as Aphra Behn or Mrs Behn she was, at times, also known as Ann Behn, Mrs Bean, agent 160 and Astrea.

Shortly after her supposed return to England from Surinam in 1664, Aphra may have married Johan Behn (also written as Johann and John Behn). He could have been a merchant of German or Dutch extraction, possibly from Hamburg. He died or the couple separated that same year, however from this point we can be sure Aphra used the title "Mrs Behn" as her professional name.

There is some suggestion that Aphra may have been a Catholic or at least leaned towards this school of faith. She once commented that she was "designed for a nun." Many of those around her were Catholic, such as Henry Neville who was later arrested for his Catholicism, and this would have aroused suspicions during the anti-Catholic fervour of the 1680s. She was a monarchist, and her sympathy for the Stuarts, and particularly for the Catholic Duke of York may be demonstrated by her dedication of her play "The Rover, Part II" to him after he had been exiled for the second time. Aphra was dedicated to the restored King Charles II. As political parties emerged during this time, Aphra became a Tory supporter.

By 1666 Aphra had become attached to the court. Domestically the Plague was sweeping the Nation and the Great Fire was about to erupt through London. In foreign affairs England and the

Netherlands had engaged in The Second Anglo-Dutch War from 1665. Aphra was recruited as a political spy in Antwerp on behalf of King Charles II, possibly in league with Thomas Killigrew.

This is probably the beginning of more accurate records on Aphra's life. Her code name is said to have been Astrea (though there are others), a name under which she later published many of her writings. Her chief duty was to establish a relationship with William Scot, son of Thomas Scot, a regicide who had been executed in 1660. Scot was believed to be ready to become a spy in the English service and to report on the activities of the English exiles who were thought to be plotting against the King. Aphra arrived in Bruges in July 1666 with a mission to secure Scot into a double agent, but there is evidence that Scot would betray her to the Dutch.

Aphra however found life as a spy not quite the romantic interlude that many assume would be the case. She arrived unprepared; the cost of living shocked her, and after a month, she had to pawn her jewellery. King Charles was slow in paying, either for her services or for her expenses whilst abroad. She had to borrow money so she could return to London, where she spent a year petitioning King Charles for payment unsuccessfully. A short while later a warrant was issued for her arrest, but little to suggest it was actually served or that she went to prison for her debt.

The death of her husband and her debts seemed to push her towards a more sustainable and substantial career. Aphra began work for the King's Company and the Duke's Company players as a scribe. These were, in fact, the only two licensed theatre groups in London. The theatres had been closed under Cromwell and were now re-opening under Charles II and a more liberal atmosphere. Theatre technology was being imported from Europe and being integrated into the staging of some plays. It was a great moment on which to embark upon a career in theatre.

Aphra who had previously only written poetry now embarked on such a career. Her first, "The Forc'd Marriage", was staged in 1670, followed by "The Amorous Prince" (1671). After her third play, "The Dutch Lover", fails to please Aphra had a three year lull in her writing career. Again it is speculated that she went travelling again, possibly once again as a spy.

After this sojourn her writing moves towards comic works, which prove commercially more successful. Her most popular works included "The Rover" and "Love-Letters Between a Nobleman and His Sister" (1684–87).

With her growing reputation Aphra became friends with many of the most notable writers of the day. This is The Age of Dryden and his literary dominance. As well as his friendship she includes also those of Elizabeth Barry, John Hoyle, Thomas Otway and Edward Ravenscroft, and was also attached to the circle of the Earl of Rochester.

Aphra often used her plays to attack the parliamentary Whigs claiming, "In public spirits call'd, good o' th' Commonwealth... So tho' by different ways the fever seize...in all 'tis one and the same mad disease." This was Aphra's criticism to parliament which had denied the king funds.

From the mid 1680's Aphra's health began to decline. This was exacerbated by her continual state of debt and descent into poverty.

In 1687 she published A Discovery of New Worlds, a translation of a French popularisation of astronomy, Entretiens sur la pluralité des mondes, by Bernard le Bovier de Fontenelle, written as a novel in a form similar to her own work, but with her new, religiously oriented preface.

As her end approached in 1689 it became increasingly hard for her to even hold a pen though her desire to continue to write was unquenchable. In her final days, she wrote the translation of the final book of Abraham Cowley's Six Books of Plants.

Aphra Behn died on April 16th 1689, and is buried in the East Cloister of Westminster Abbey. The inscription on her tombstone reads: "Here lies a Proof that Wit can never be Defence enough against Mortality." She was quoted as stating that she had led a "life dedicated to pleasure and poetry."

Her legacy is broad. Firstly as a woman she broke down many of the barriers which regarded only men as writers, especially in the commercial arena. In all she would write and have performed 19 plays, contribute to more, and become one of the first prolific, high-profile female dramatists in these Isles.

In her own golden age of the 1670s and 1680s she was one of the most productive playwrights in Britain, second only to the immense talents of the Poet Laureate John Dryden.

Much of her work has been criticised for its bawdy tone as well as its masculine form but needs must and she was working to live, to survive, and to widen her spread as an author.

She received widespread support from many other successful writers including Thomas Otway, Nahum Tate (also a Poet Laureate), Jacob Tonson, Nathaniel Lee and Thomas Creech.

Aphra is now rightly seen as a key dramatist of the seventeenth-century theatre. Her prose vitally important to the on-going development of the English novel.

Following Aphra's death new female dramatists such as 'Ariadne', Delarivier Manley, Mary Fix, Susanna Centlivre and Catherine Trotter acknowledged Behn as an inspiration who opened up the public space for women writers to be accepted.

In succeeding centuries her appreciation has been volatile. For instance in the morally reserved Victorian clime both the writer and her works were ignored or dismissed as indecent. The Victorian novelist and critic Julia Kavanagh wrote, "the disgrace of Aphra Behn is that, instead of raising man to woman's moral standard, she sank woman to the level of man's coarseness".

However by the 20th century, however, Aphra's fame was back in fashion. Since then her works have been well appreciated and her place in our literary pantheon assured.

Aphra Behn – A Concise Bibliography

Plays
The Forced Marriage (1670)
The Amorous Prince (1671)
The Dutch Lover (1673)
Abdelazer (1676)
The Town Fop (1676)
The Rover, Part I (1677)
Sir Patient Fancy (1678)
The Feigned Courtesans (1679)
The Young King (1679)

The False Count (1681)
The Rover, Part II (1681)
The Roundheads (1681)
The City Heiress (1682)
Like Father, Like Son (1682)
Prologue and Epilogue to Romulus and Hersilia, or The Sabine War (November 1682)
The Lucky Chance (1686) with composer John Blow
The Emperor of the Moon (1687)
The Widow Ranter (1689)
The Younger Brother (1696)

Novels
The Fair Jilt
Agnes de Castro
Love-Letters Between a Nobleman and His Sister (1684)
Oroonoko (1688)

Short Stories
The Fair Jilt (1688)
The History of the Nun: or, the Fair Vow-Breaker (1688)
The History of the Servant
The Lover-Boy of Germany
The Girl Who Loved the German Lover-Boy

Poetry Collections
Poems upon Several Occasions, with A Voyage to the Island of Love (1684)
Lycidus; or, The Lover in Fashion (1688)

The Dorset Square Theatre – A Short History

Many of Aphra Behn's plays were first performed at the Dorset Garden Theatre in London which was originally built in 1671.

The theatre itself is rich in history though it survived for less than forty years. In its first years it was also commonly called the Duke of York's Theatre, as well as the Duke's Theatre. Charles II died in 1685 and his brother the Duke of York was crowned King James II. The theatre then changed its name to The Queen's Theatre in honour of James' wife Mary of Modena.

It was the fourth home of the Duke's Company, one of the two patent theatre companies in Restoration London, and after 1682 continued to be used by the company's successor, the United Company.

After the Civil war and the harsh years of the Interregnum the ban on theatres was lifted with the Restoration of Charles II in 1660. He granted Letters Patent to two theatre companies. One enjoyed his own patronage, this was 'The King's Company'. The other was patronised by his brother the Duke of York and was known as The Duke's Company.

Both were originally based in the Cockpit Theatre, an old Jacobean theatre in Drury Lane. The Duke's Company then moved for a short time to the Salisbury Court Theatre and thence in 1662 to

Portugal Street in Lincoln's Inn Fields remaining there until 1671. The King's Company meanwhile moved to the Theatre Royal, Drury Lane.

Sir William Davenant, the respected Poet Laureate, founded the Duke's company and brought much innovation to theatre especially with regard to changeable scenery and theatrical machinery. Davenant died on April 7th 1668. He had made plans for a new theatre but died before ground was broken on the new theatre in 1670. This was funded to the tune of £9,000 by the Davenant family, the theatre's leading actor Thomas Betterton and others. A site was leased in Dorset Square under a 39 year lease at a rent of £130.55 per annum.

The theatre opened in the following year with the return of Thomas Betterton to England from a trip to France. It is thought that Betterton had gone several times over the years to bring back French thinking and equipment and certainly this seems evident with the Company's elaborate productions, including operatic adaptations of Shakespeare's Macbeth (1673), The Tempest (1674), and Thomas Shadwell's Pysche (1675). These productions employed changeable perspective scenery moved by machines as well as for flying actors and objects

The site of the theatre, was in the former grounds of Dorset House, London seat of the Sackville Earls of Dorset. Destroyed in the Great Fire of London it was soon densely built over with speculative tenements. It appears part of the site had been used as a theatre in the time of Charles I: in 1629 the Earl of Dorset leased the "stables and out howses towards the water side" behind Dorset House... to make a playhouse for the children of the revels."

The site for the new theatre, by Dorset Stairs in Whitefriars on the Thames, was slightly upstream from the outlet of the New Canal, part of the Fleet River. Its position on the Thames permitted the patrons to travel to the theatre by boat, avoiding the nearby crime-ridden neighbourhood of Alsatia. It opened on 9 November 1671 and was almost twice the size of the Duke's Company's former theatre. It became the principal playhouse in London when the Theatre Royal burned down in January 1672, and only rivalled when the new Theatre Royal opened in March 1674.

After the Duke's Company merged with the King's Company in 1682 to form the United Company, the theatre in Dorset Garden was used mainly for opera, music, and spectaculars. From the 1690s it was used as well for other entertainments, such as weight lifting, until it was demolished in 1709. Apart from the illustrations in the libretto of The Empress of Morocco, no contemporary pictures of the interior are known. It is thought that the interior was richly decorated: the proscenium arch had carvings by Grinling Gibbons.

The Dorset Garden theatre, typically for English theatres, had a large forestage. Edward Langhans in his reconstruction calculated the forestage to be 19'6" feet deep and 30'6" wide at the proscenium arch. This forestage provided actors, singers and dancers with a sizeable downstage and a well lit performance space, free of grooves. When a locale was depicted by the scenery, the forestage was understood to be an extension of that place and served as the link between the audience and the performers, the auditorium and the stage, the playgoers and the play.

Access to the forestage was by proscenium doors, probably two on each side of the stage. Above the doors were balconies; acting spaces that could also serve for seating.

The scenic stage was probably some 50' deep and 30' high. The proscenium arch may have been some 30' wide and at least 25' high to accommodate the scenery in operas such as Dioclesian, The Fairy-Queen, or The World in the Moon. Both the forestage and the scenic stage were raked.

The music box above the proscenium arch could hold perhaps 8 to 10 musicians, to provide incidental music. A full orchestra would be sitting in the pit, just in front of the stage.

The Duke's Company had already been using moveable scenery to good effect in their previous playhouses. It was first employed by Davenant at Rutland House, using shutters in grooves, which could be slid open or closed to reveal a new scene. However Dorset Garden was also equipped to fly at least four separate people and large objects like a cloud covering the full width of the stage and carrying a large group of musicians (such as in Psyche 1675). There were also numerous floor traps. It was primarily designed for staging Restoration spectaculars, and was the only playhouse in London capable of all the effects these lavish and exuberant spectacles required.

It is not known who designed the new theatre building. On the outside it measured 148' by 57', including a 10' deep porch.

A foreign visitor reported in 1676 that it contained a central "pit", in the form of an amphitheatre, two tiers of seven boxes each holding twenty people, and an upper gallery. In all the theatre could entertain 850 people at a time. The theatre represented a great investment to the Duke's Company. Thomas Betterton lived in an apartment on an upper floor on the south side. And living nearby were such luminaries as Aphra Behn in Dorset Street; John Dryden in Salisbury Square (from 1673 to 1682) and John Locke in Dorset Court in 1690.

www.ingramcontent.com/pod-product-compliance
Lightning Source LLC
Chambersburg PA
CBHW061456040426
42450CB00007B/1377